Letters to
Santa Claus

Letters to Santa Claus

The ELVES

Foreword by Pat Koch, Head Elf
Afterword by Emily Weisner Thompson

INDIANA UNIVERSITY PRESS

Bloomington & Indianapolis

This book is a publication of

Indiana University Press
Office of Scholarly Publishing
Herman B Wells Library 350
1320 East 10th Street
Bloomington, Indiana 47405 USA

iupress.indiana.edu

The paper used in this publication meets the minimum requirements of the American National Standard for Information Sciences—Permanence of Paper for Printed Library Materials, ANSI Z39.48–1992.

Manufactured in China

Cataloging information is available from the Library of Congress.

ISBN 978-0-253-01793-2 (cloth)
ISBN 978-0-253-01794-9 (ebook)

1 2 3 4 5   20 19 18 17 16 15

To all of Santa's Elves:

Without you,
there would be no magic.

Contents

Pat Yellig Koch and her brother, Ray Yellig Jr., at the 1935 Santa Statue (circa 1941).

Photo courtesy Santa Claus Museum & Village.

DEDICATED
TO THE CHILDREN OF THE WORLD
IN
MEMORY OF AN UNDYING LOVE
DEC 25 1935

Foreword

Head Elf
Pat Koch has
been helping
Santa answer
letters since
she was twelve
years old.

As Santa's daughter, I have a special appreciation for Christmas. Growing up near the southern Indiana town of Santa Claus only deepened this feeling. In Santa Claus, Indiana, the spirit of Christmas is a gift we experience all year round. Our little town is home to a thriving community of about 2,300 residents who live on streets named Mistletoe and Rudolph, eat lunch at Frosty's or St. Nick's, and shop for groceries at Holiday Foods. To the casual observer, we may simply appear as a quirky place that clearly enjoys the Christmas season. But dig a little deeper, and you'll realize there is more to Christmas in Santa Claus than festive names and candy-striped street crossings. This community takes pride in its traditions and holds a legacy that dates back over one hundred and fifty years.

My father's full name was Raymond Joseph Yellig, and he didn't just play Santa Claus—he *was* Santa Claus. It was his calling, his passion, his mission. He was born in 1894 in the small town of Mariah Hill, Indiana, about four

Above: Children sit at antique school desks in the Original Santa Claus Post Office and write their letters to Santa.

Photo courtesy Spencer County Visitors Bureau.

Below: Holly the Elf sorts the Christmas mail in the Original Santa Claus Post Office.

Photo courtesy Santa Claus Museum & Village.

miles north of Santa Claus. He served in the Navy during World War I, and while stationed in Brooklyn, New York, he was asked to play Santa Claus at a party his ship hosted for underprivileged children in the neighborhood. Being a boy from a town called Santa Claus, it seemed like a perfect fit. My father loved the experience and prayed to God that if he made it through the war, he would forever be Santa Claus.

He did, indeed, survive the war and returned home to marry his childhood sweetheart, my mother, Isabelle. My father took his vow seriously and spent his life as Santa Jim Yellig. He worked at Santa Claus Land (today known as Holiday World & Splashin' Safari) for nearly forty years and listened to the Christmas wishes of over one million children. He appeared in radio programs, parades, print ads, and game shows. He was truly the face of Santa Claus, Indiana, for many, many years.

My father started helping the postmaster of Santa Claus, James Martin, in 1930. Every year, children from across the United States mailed their letters to Santa Claus, and those letters turned up in Santa Claus, Indiana. Postmaster Martin was trying to respond to every letter that arrived. He needed help, and my father was more than happy to give it. He'd bring boxes of letters home, and years after his death, I was still finding letters he'd answered scattered throughout the house. He was

one of the greatest men I've ever known. "Happiness is what it's all about," he once said. "I make kids happy."

I've always tried to take this lesson to heart. My own involvement with the Santa letters began in 1944. I started helping my father answer letters when I was twelve years old. I remember my mother admonishing him to move the tablecloth out of the way before he upended bags of letters and started writing—she didn't want ink all over her furniture.

I grew up, moved away, and thought my life had taken a completely different turn. But my father grew ill, and I returned to southern Indiana to help where I could. Bill Koch, whose father had started Santa Claus Land, picked me up at the train station, and we were married in 1960. Together, he and I devoted our lives to Santa Claus Land and the town of Santa Claus, where we raised our five children. I've lived most of my life in or near this Christmas town, where children from around the world still send their most heartfelt desires, and I know how truly special it is to live in a small town where the Christmas spirit surrounds you every day.

I have always believed in the importance of preserving history. I founded the Santa Claus Museum in 2006 to preserve and interpret the history of Santa Claus, Indiana, and filled it with a collection of wonderful photographs, artifacts, and Santa Claus Land memorabilia that documents the history of our town.

Eventually, our little museum outgrew its original location in Kringle Place and moved to a spot in the old town of Santa Claus, adjacent to the giant Santa Claus statue, which was built in 1935. In addition to the museum and statue, the new location is also home to the historic 1880 Deutsch Evangelische St. Paul's Kirche (or Santa Claus Church) and the Original Santa Claus Post Office from 1856.

Above, left: Each year Santa's Elves respond to thousands of letters from children all over the world. Here, Head Elf Pat Koch keeps an eye on the workshop.

Above, right: Head Elf Pat Koch helps Santa by responding to one of the thousands of letters mailed to Santa Claus, Indiana, every year. She's wearing her best Christmas attire!

Photos courtesy Spencer County Visitors Bureau.

Below: The Original Santa Claus Post Office in the Snow.

Photo courtesy Kendell Thompson.

Relocated several times before coming to rest at the Santa Claus Museum & Village, the post office is a wonderful space where visitors can still get a sense of how letters for Santa arrived a hundred years ago. Though the building has not been used as a post office since the late 1800s, it has been renovated to resemble the old-fashioned post office it once was. Today, children can sit at antique school desks and write their letters to Santa Claus. And in the back, another group gathers to answer them—letter after letter.

The Original Santa Claus Post Office serves as the headquarters for Santa's Elves, a non-profit group that merged with the museum in 2006. Each Christmas season, a dedicated cadre of volunteer elves gathers to help Santa answer all of the letters that arrive in town each year. It is a continuation of the tradition started by James Martin and kept alive by subsequent postmasters, by my father, Santa Jim, and now by me.

As I grow older, the importance of remembering our history and where we came from looms large in my mind. I realize how essential traditions are. I am proud of what our town has accomplished and incredibly grateful to all of the elves who donate so much time each year to ensure that each and every child who writes a letter to Santa Claus receives a response.

If you stop by the Santa Claus Museum, you'll see an exhibit featuring letters to Santa Claus sent from children around the world. Thanks to this book, you can now take home some of our favorites—maybe there's even one here from your grandmother or grandfather. I am excited to share our collection of wonderful letters with you and wish you a very Merry Christmas, all year long.

Pat Koch

Holly the Elf tidies up the Original Santa Claus Post Office after a busy day of helping children write their letters to Santa Claus.
Photo courtesy Kendell Thompson.

Acknowledgments

This book has been a long time coming. Thank you so much to Indiana University Press for making it happen. Thank you to Holiday World & Splashin' Safari for your generous donations that continue to support the efforts of Santa's Elves. Thank you to Pat Koch, for your tireless devotion to preserving the history of Santa Claus, Indiana, and for continuing the tradition of Santa's Elves. To the Board of Directors at the Santa Claus Museum & Village, thank you for your support and guidance. Thank you to our neighbors, friends, and community in and around Santa Claus, Indiana—you are the keepers of our traditions. Most of all, thank you to all of my volunteer elves. Your gift of time during the busy holiday season is appreciated more than you know.

EMILY WEISNER THOMPSON

Letters to
Santa Claus

Dear Santa Claus

Please bring for me a pair of warm gloves and for John a pair of shoes size 1 and for Claire some warm underwear and for Joe stocking size 10 and for Rose gloves for 12 years old becaus we are poor and got no money for toys or candy Pleas come to our house as I will be waiting for you Jimmie aint so good so if you want you could leave him out — he is 10 years old. Mama is fat but she never wants anything for christmas

We are Rose 12
Joe 11
James 10
Catherine 9
John 8
Claire 7
and the others are
dead. I hope I get them
what I ask for Catherine colrs
Dairs are
Woodstock md.

Mr. Scott Miller
Diller Nebr.

Postmaster
Santa Claus
Indiana

DILLER
DEC
3
11 PM
1935
NEBR

CHRISTMAS
1935

Diller Nebr.
Nov 22, 1935

Dear Santa Claus,
    How are you? Is it cold at
the north pole? Does
the wind blow through
your whiskers? I am a little
girl seven years old. I
would like to have a blue
tricycle for Christmas. also
a Shirley Temple book and a
dolworth rubber pants. I
hope my doll can say
mama. I wish it could
open and shut it's eyes.
Don't forget the little
poor children. They need
a merry Christmas too.
With much love and kiss.
To the jolliest fellow in
the world. I am lovingly
yours.
                Gloria Joyce Miller

Gilman,
Wis.

Dear Santa Claus:
        Grandma Joyce said
she heard on the radio
that you would send us kids
some thing for Christmas
this year. We have been
good kids and helped Daddy
and Mother. Some times we
were bad but we didn'
mean to. Could we have
some candy and nuts this
year?
        Good - by Santa Claus.
Catherine Joyce 10 Years,
James 9   Richard 5
Eileen 7   Jeanette 2
Robert 6   Virginia 8mo.

Annapolis, Mo.
Dec. 12th 1939.

Dear Santa Claus

I am a pretty big boy 12 years old some of my pals say there is no Santa but I just have to believe in him and I'm hoping he will not forget me.

My dad was a soldier in the World war. He got shot when he was a deputy sherriff by gangsters after he come back.

I have a step dad but he is so mean he never buys me anything. Some day I will be a man and I want to be brave. I like books better than anything and I like boxing gloves & foot balls.

I hope you answer my letter.

Your friend
Wilson Castile Jr.
Annapolis, Mo.

Port Arthur Tx.
Dec 16 1935

Dear Santa:
I am a boy 7 years old.
I don't wont much.
Mother has already sent
you the money for a
tool chest and foot ball.
Please don't forget me.
you may find some thing
to eat in the ice box when
you come.

love to you.
Harley Maxwell

Please answer consenting
to bring these Articles.
Mrs. C. L. Maxwell
Port Arthur Texas

Love
        Ellen

Dear Santa
    wrap yourself
    up good so you
    wont catch cold.

Ellen Mariner

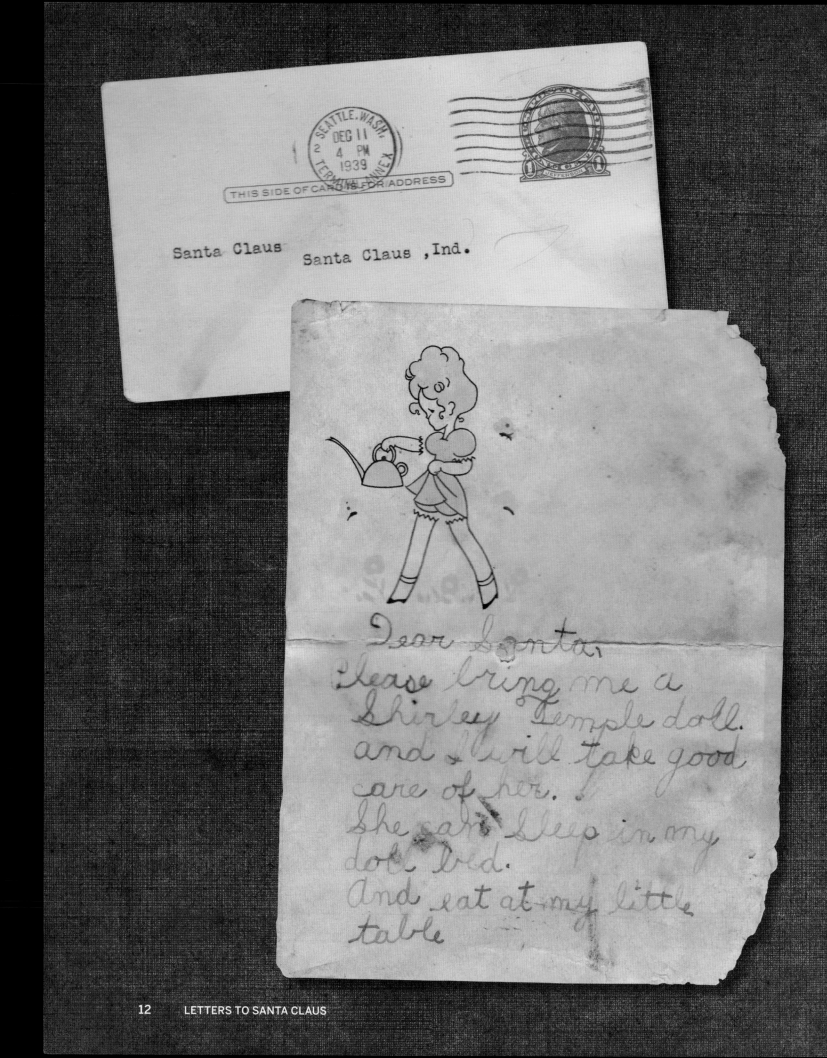

THIS SIDE OF CARD IS FOR ADDRESS

Santa Claus

Santa Claus ,Ind.

Dear Santa,
Please bring me a
Shirley Temple doll.
and I will take good
care of her.
She can sleep in my
doll bed.
And eat at my little
table

Dear Santa Clause

as my Daddy not working
and I will not get nothing
for chirstmas.
I would like very much
for a Sherly timply doll
I am six years old and
will be seven years
old april, 17
Santa don't forget me
Send to
Betty Jane Walker
Swiss West
Virgnia

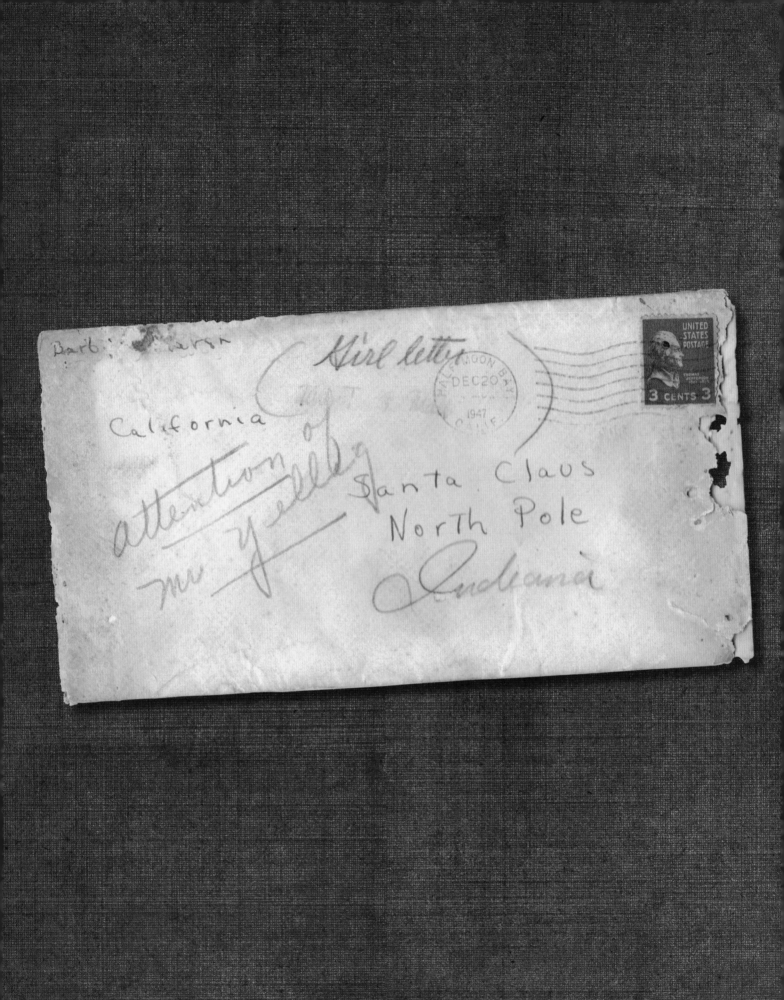

December 19, 1947

Santa Claus
North Pole

Dear Santa:

In making this plea I am hoping
you still remember the days when you
were young before you had met Mrs.
Claus. Remember how your heart
used to get fluttery when you saw a
pretty girl? Remember the times you
had crushes on those smilin' misses?
Ah, love! And then you met Mrs. Claus —
Remember how you used to hold hands
and swing on the garden gate and how
sweet and thrilled she looked when
you tasted her first biscuit, (the
one that gave you chronic indigestion?)
Remember the love notes you used to
pass? Ah! ain't love grand? Ah, yes!
Well, Santa, I'm in a heck of a fix
right now. Here it is only twelve
days before the new year starts
and I'm without a man! Isn't
that a horrible predicament to be in?!
There's another gal here in the same

2

boat with me. Her name is Velma and
we each want a man for Christmas.
Couldn't you please look around to
see if there are any spare ones
up there?? I'd be awfully happy if
you would. Just in case there's
plenty to choose from, I'm sending
a general description of our preferred
choices.

I want one who's about 5'4"
or 5"5", or 5'6" or 5'7" or 5'8"
or 5'9" with wavy or curly hair that
is striped brown and blond. Make
him about 20 and let him have
a black club coupe with white
wall tires to come down in. Just
give him my address and send
him right out. I'll be waiting!!

Velma wants a guy with blue
glass eyes, very tanned complexion,
and a friendly disposition. She'd
appreciate it if he was about as
young as Larry Watts, our loco
postmaster, with a straight blond

3 wig which he keeps trimmed down to a crew cut, and a firm, straight jaw, with a strong nose, (not quite as strong as an elephant's though.) She'd like him to be about 6'6" or more, with size 14½ shoes. She said to send him in a hearse, (not in back, either!!)

As an added precaution, we both agree: Just send us some males. That's all we're asking for this year, so don't you think you could bring us what we want just this once? Gee, thanks a million, Santa. We're sure grateful and we'll be waiting!

Sincerely,
Barbara Marsh

P.S. Could mine have dimples?

11/18/48

                                                   Marin

County, California

Dear Santa Claus,
        I have been a good boy. May I please
have a toy road scraper? May I please have a
cooking set to help my mother? May I please
have a baseball mit? May I please have a
drum?
        I will leave a glass of water, and a
glass and a bottle opener and a bottle of
beer, and a liverworst sandwich on a
plate, and a glass of milk on the mantle
for you.
        Thank you very much.

                ALD HA RA
                SIMS

(as dictated by
Richard Sims)

Dear Santa:

Please send Louise Hinkle a pair of Nylon
Stockings.   They will be deeply appreciated.

Wishing you a Merry Christmas and Happy New
Year, I am

                    Sororally yours,

                        An Admirer

Cincinnati Ohio
Dec-1st '40

Dear Mr Santa Clause :-   I told my daddy
there wasn't any Santa Clause and he to me
to write to you so if you answer this card
I will know there is a real Santa Clause
                        Yours Respt
                        Catherine Procter
                        Cinti Ohio

DEAR SANTA CLAUS

I'M A REAL GOOD GIRL SO
BRING ME SOME SPURS AND
SOME TOYS, AND A WHITE
COWBOY HAT. I LIKE TO PLAY
ROY ROGERS. I'M ALMOST
FOUR YEARS OLD.
THANK YOU SANTA

LYLENE

TYLER, TEXAS

P.S.
MY MOTHER HELPED ME WRITE THIS.
THIS IS MY PART

© WALT DISNEY PRODUCTIONS

Dear Santa,
For Christmas I want a dumptruck,
digger, doctor set, electric train,
and football. I guess that is all
I want for Christmas.

All my Love to
Santie

Roy   Age 4

Scottsburg, Ind.

P. S. I hope none of your reindeers
get sick so you won't miss
my house. And don't miss it.

I know you are very busy with your Christmas mail but I shall be waiting to hear from you.

Sincerely yours,
Malcolm

Watertown,
Mass.

Dec. 9, 1947

Dear Postmaster,

Just a few minutes ago I heard via the radio how a woman wrote to you in search of a husband for a Christmas present. I think I have the man.

He is tall, stately, well-bred, a man of wealth with a steady income from his real estate. Although there are a few gray hairs beneath his hat, he wears them well. A smile on his face, money in his pockets—what more could a woman ask for?

Widow Asks Santa For A New Husband

SANTA CLAUS, Ind., Dec. 13.—(NANA)—A 47-year-old Columbus, O., widow today added her Christmas wants to the appeals of 35,000 children who have written letters to Santa Claus.

In a letter received here at Santa Claus, Ind., she wrote:

"I want a good husband for Christmas."

She hopes her future mate will be found "on a farm right inside Indiana," and her letter pleads with Santa to have the man "write me at once so that I may really be his Christmas-gift wife."

Dear Santa

In Request To your reply To a widow of 47 for a husband for a christmas present I would like to hear from her as I have lost my wife and This lady is about my age as I am only 50 years myself and I live on a farm of 80 acres

Mr Elmer

Ridgeway
Ohio

Ocean Park Calif
Dec 14 - 47

Nana
Columbus Ohio
Dear Nana I see a clipping In the Los Angeles Examiner That your Put in your request For a Husband from Santa Well Now you Just send me a Snap Shot of your self. And we will try and see If your are the girl of my Dreams I am a Widower too been a sod Widower for seven years Now I am a Hoosier my self from Bedford and you might want to live out here In California I am Just a Working man for air Craft Co. Been with them 5 years now make $1.00 Per Hour So If I am the Lucky one you Pick out of all the letter you get See be Lucky your Truly

Arthur

Ocean Park Calif

wants a little horse
that he can wheel around
as he is walking.

Please bring me what
you can won't you
Santa Claus. I have just
started school last
Easter, and now gone
into another class.

~~Hoping~~ Hoping to hear from
you.

Yours Sincerely
Edna
Castleton Age
5 yrs.

x x x x x.

Lowestoft
Suffolk
England.
2·8·49.

Dear Santa Claus.
I am a little girl
of 5 yrs old, and I
would like a big dolly
with open & shut eyes,
and talks, also a ball
& some books. My daddy
doesn't earn very much
money, and I have asked
my mummy to write to
you. I have a little sister
of 2½ yrs, and she wants
a dolly's pram & dolly, and
my little brother of 1yr 3mths

NUMBER	BULLETIN
400	
401	
402	
403	
404	
405	
406	
407	
408	
409	
410	
411	
412	
413	
414	
415	
416	
417	
418	
419	
420	
421	
422	
423	
424	
425	
426	
427	
428	
429	
430	
431	
432	
433	
434	
435	
436	
437	
438	
439	
440	

Dear Santa,

I have been a pretty good boy all this year. Please bring me a wagon (since my Daddy hit mine with the car and it is now pink), a truck, a dump, some blocks, train cars, lawn mower and a tractor, a barn & house, & cow, Yours Truly,

Billy

CINDERELLA

HANSEL AND GRETEL

Powell Oregon
Dec. 27, 194_

Dear Santa Claus
I am glad

you recieved my
letter. I would
like to see the
brownies. They would
look cute, I'm sure.
Would you send me
a picture of them

SLEEPING BEAUTY

SNOW WHITE

at work, please?
I would like it
very much. Thank
you for the nice
gifts you gave
me. How old
are you? Write
 me soon, please.
Your Friend Maria
Hartzell
P.S. I am 9
years old.

Dear Santa,

I would like skis, ski boots, ski poles, ski harnesses, for Christmas. I think of you every day in school. I hope you will send me the things I wrote on the letter. Pleas send me skis, ski boots, ski poles, and ski harnesses. My arm is getting tired. I guess I have to go now. Good-by.

With love,
David

SAINT JOHNSBURY
NOV 18
4 PM
1948
VT.

UNITED STATES POSTAGE
THOMAS JEFFERSON 1801-1809
3 CENTS 3

Santa Claus
North pole

Patty made these decorations

S A N T A S

Dear Santa,
Please get me a scooter
a duck toy and please try to
find me a penguin. Bring me
Pammy a dolly. Please bring
some candy, nuts and
oranges.

PROTECT YOUR STAMPS, PHOTOGRAPHS AND COLOR PRINTS

1947
MERRY CHRISTMAS

Dec. 12, 1947.

Dear Santa Claus:

I'm writing this letter for my son Robert Jr. who is one year old. He has seen one of your helpers at Gimbels Dept. Store and wanted a stuffed toy for Xmas.

Enclosed is a picture of my son watching at the fireplace for Santa Claus to come.

Thank you Santa

Bob
for
Son Jr.

Dec 16, 1951

Dear Santa Claus

I am writing to tell you and your Staff
that this year I've been a stinker - a real louse.
So dont bother to bring me a thing.
Heres what I mean;

JAN. — Put tobasco Sauce on Ice Cream.
My Brother thought it was Hersheys Syrup.
Then The Fun Began.

FEB. Put an Imitation Snake on Ma's
Dresser. - We Had to Revive Ma — Then Aunt
Nellie Fainted - and we revived her. Then
Sis Fainted — Gee Santa - we Had a
real revival Meeting!

MARCH — Im a Generous guy at Heart
Santa - I Just gave my Kid brother
the Mumps.

APRIL — My Big Sister - (she's 14) - Went
out on her first date with some

(OVER)

jerk. — I put itching powder in all her clothes just before she left (Including her underwear.)

MAY — I just couldn't resist putting the garter snake down Ma's neck. Sure was funny—for a while!

JUNE — Only a week left of School. I couldn't resist setting off the fire Alarm. —Gee, Santa—Did that joint empty fast! (Our School principal aint got no Sence of Hoomer !!!!)

JULY— A Bunch of gals took over our 'ole Swimmin' Hole.—Being a cub Scout I practiced tying Knots in their clothes. After wetting them of course.

AUG.— At the Sunday School Picnic. I Pushed Percival Pantywilles Puss into the Jello—I got spanked—but It was worth it!

3) Sept — School Started again. Before
School I went to a painless Dentist
— He was a Fake — I bit his thumb and
he yelled just like anyone else!

Oct. — Halloween — I tipped over many
of those small buildings with the
Crescent Moon on the Door. — Funny, but
I thought I heard a scream from
inside one of Them. — But I was
too big a Hurry to investigate.

Nov. — at the school Party — I pushed
Prisilla Pinkertons Pretty Pink Puss into
the Pumpkin Pie — No one else
approved — but I havent had such
fun since I fed the neighbors cat
Castor Oil.''

Dec. — I Didnt Do much This month
yet — Santa — But give me time
I still got 2 weeks
(OVER

So you see Santa, I Dont deserve anything — But just bring peace on Earth and Stop these damn Wars — and all of us will be Happy.

P. S — Dont drive your Reindeer over our House Buster — With the price of beef what it is, and pappys shotgun so Conveniently Handy, — Well ——

Anyhow Santa
Merry Christmas!

Snodgrass Schnootie
The good little Bad Boy

Santa Claus
North Pole or
Ind.

Rush — Personal

Dear Santa Claus.
    please will you
bring me a 20 ton
lorry-mounted crane,
And a foden flat truck
with tailboard, also a
euclid rear dump truck,
and I would like a
mersey tunnel Police Varr.
I will have anything you
care to bring me. I hope
you are very well.

I wish you a merry
xmas and to all your
elves, Love from Stuart.
XXXX XXXX XXXXXXXXX

Dear Santa

I would like to be an elf because I work really hard and I can paint and color real good.

I can sew and knit scarves real good and I can read good.

I can draw things and I would help pack the things and write down the names on the list.

I would wrap presents for you.

I would get the reindeer in order for you.

I would get the candy all ready for the trip.

Love,
Alana

6/12/50

May

Renfrew
Scotland

Dear Scanta Claus

  I got your lovely letter today and I thank
you verry much, I was wondering if you
had got mine as its such a long time
since I sent it, I though you must
be busy, you will be sorry to hear
my Dady has been verry ill for a
lot of months now, and my big Brother
is still in hospital that all this year,
and my other Brother got some papers
and had to go to sea he is a second
Engenure in the Clan Boat, so we wont
be having much fun this year as
my mother has not much money so
I will just take what you send me
even if it only some ribbon and
hankies I dont mind as I know mother
will get me something nice when
my dady goes to work again I say
my prayers every night and ask
Jesus to make him better, and I
pray for you as well you are
so kind and I ask him to let
me get something nice for christmas

and I know he will some how
becaurse my mother and dady
say y we ask him and its good
for us he will let us have it
so I have told him to let me
have something nice, I am elevan
now and I helh mother all I
can, oh scanta will you please
take this presant and keep it
for yourself please as you have
been so kind to me and I would
like you to have it my mother
said I may let you have it I
hope some of the other children
remember to send you something
for beying so kind to them, well
santa dear its be time so I must
say good night and God Bless
you a merry christmas and
a happy new year
your ever loving we friend

May

xxxxxxxx +
by by your house is a lovely
one

Chgo, Illinois
Nov. 5, 1953

Dear Santa Claus:

You must help us this year Santa, our daddy still doesn't come home and mama cries at night when she thinks we are asleep, because she has no money for our coats and shoes and some dolls for Christmas

Sister says Santa Claus would help if he knew so I am writing you early so you can read this before Christmas.

Junior wants Gene autry guns he is 4 years old.
Duffy is the baby she is 2 she can't talk
Mechele wants a piano she is 5
Michael is 3, he wants a truck
Don't give me anything but give

my mother some shoes please
with the heels on like the other
ladies she wears sock and I
like stockings on the pretty
ladies I see. I am 8 years
old but if you can I would
like a pretty coat like the
other girls have on.

Father William said pray
and I do, but do you think
he heard me.

Shyrle

Chicago, Illinois

P.S we go see you every year
and I called you up
once.

Shyrle

CHICAGO
NOV 7
6 10 PM
1953

Santa Claus
North Pole
or Mich, Ind.

Dear Santa Claus,
    The following is the list of things I
would like for Christmas:
A tonner fifty.
A Winchester Rifle
A Buckle gun-Belt.
A watch.
A firetruck that shoots water.
A Cartruck.

    Clark

Tell City Ind.
Oct. 27, 1959.

16/10/55

J. M.
ACRE PLACE
PLYMOUTH

DEAR SANTA CLAUS,
            IF YOU
CAN FIND ROOM IN YOUR
BAG I SHOULD LIKE A
HIGH CHAIR FOR MY
DOLLY AND A ROCKING
CRADLE TO.
PLEASE EXCUSE MY
WRITING I AM ONLY
6 AND IT ISNT VERY
EASY YET.
            LOVE
        JENNIFER.

Curundu, C. Z.
Dec. 5th, 1950.

Dear Santa Claus:
                    I have been a good
boy and I want to you to bring me a few
things:
        A tool chest, a tank, an airplane,
2 guns and spurs, a record player, a pet
of little soldiers, a bicycle, a horse puzzle,
a gasoline station with extra cars, a parachute &
a rubber hunting knife.

That's is all, if, I remember, anything else I
will write and tell you.
                            Bye
                        Georgie

19. 08. 55.

Dear Santa Claus!

I'm a little girl 5 years.
My mother and father are displaced
pisions and they can't buy me all
I'm wishing.
But I will hang my
stocking over the fire-place. There will
be a present in it for you. Will
you please bring me a doll other
anything you will.
I thank you very much
and wish you merry christmas
with love
from
MARE

Mare
Dr. Sandburgig.
Nybro / Sweden

1960s

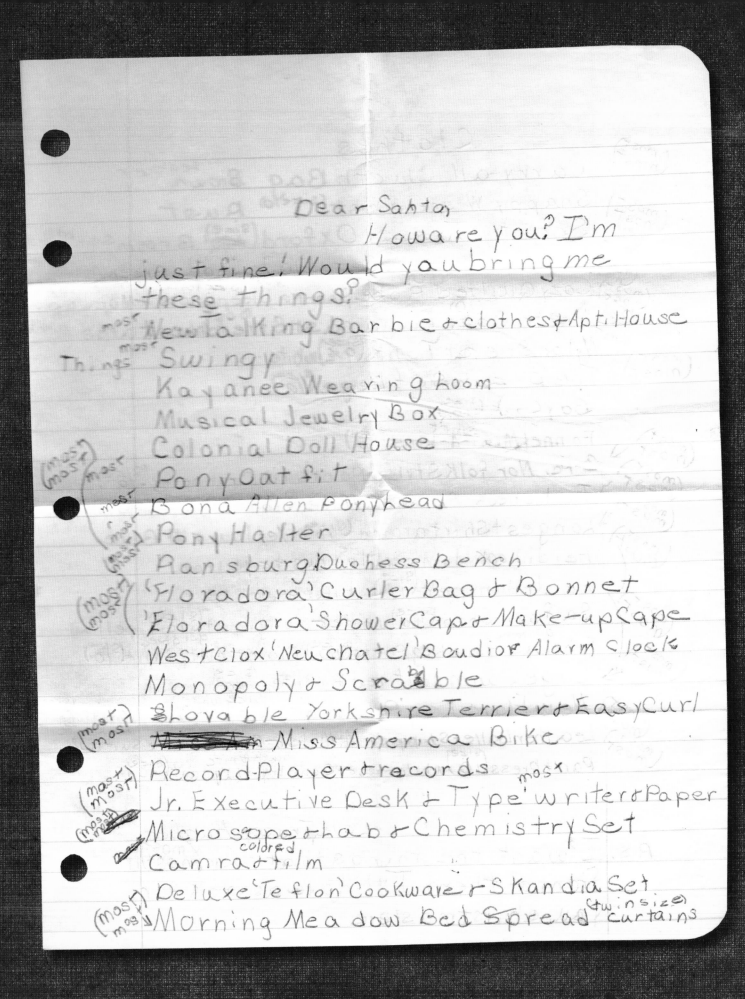

Dear Santa,
How are you? I'm just fine! Would you bring me these things?

(most) New Talking Barbie & clothes & Apt. House
(most) Things Swingy
Kayanee Wearing Loom
Musical Jewelry Box
(most)(most) Colonial Doll House
(most) Pony Outfit
(most) Bona Allen Pony Head
(most)(most) Pony Halter
Aansburg Duchess Bench
(most)(most) 'Floradora' Curler Bag & Bonnet
'Floradora' Shower Cap & Make-up Cape
West Clox 'Neuchatel' Boudior Alarm Clock
Monopoly & Scrabble
(most)(most) Lovable Yorkshire Terrier & Easy Curl
(most)(most) ~~An~~ Miss America Bike
(most)(most) Record Player & records
(most) Jr. Executive Desk & Type'writer & Paper most
(most)(most) Microscope & Lab & Chemistry Set
(most) Camra & film colored
(most) Deluxe 'Teflon' Cookware & Skandia Set
(most) Morning Meadow Bed Spread (twin size) curtains

Clothes

(most/most) Carry-all Clucth Bag Brown leather

(most/most) Snappy Western Vest (size 10) Rust

(most/most) Sporty Tassel Oxford (size ~~10~~) Brown smooth

most (most/most) Lovely Lingerie Set (size 10) (bras 30) Green

(most/most) Cozy Quilted Robe Short & Sleep Boots & Mop Cap most (size 10)

Be Pretty Cozy Pajamas (10) & Stretch Leotards M. White most

most (most/most) Nylon Stretch Tights (size 9½) white

(most/most) The Drizzle Suit Beige (size 10)

Boy Coat (size 10)

Fannel Mini-A-Line Skirt (size 10)

(most/most) 3-Pc. Nor folk Styled Pantsuit Cranberry (size 10)

(most/most) Turtleneck Pullover White (size 10)

(most/most) Longest Shirt around (size 10) Yellow & ~~B~~ Blue

(most/most) Heidi Look Jumper (size 10) rust & yellow

Heidi Jumper (size 10) blue & white

(most/most) Safari Shop (size 10) white & Long Vest (size 10) yellow gold & red gold & red

(most/most) Fabolous Flare Leg Pants (size 10) Plaid & Kilty Skirt (size 10)

(most/most) Cage Swimsuit red & white (size 10)

(most/most) New Flare Leg Pants ankle (size 10) & Nifty Knit Tops (size 10) white red & white

(most/most) Leather Ballet Slipper M. White & 2-Pc. Minimate Suit (10) blue & white

Pant Dress (10) white & red & Country Playsuit (size 10)

Love, Tracey

P.S. I want the things that have (most) in front of them. I'll have a snack for you chirstmas eve.

Columbiana,
Alabama
Oct. - 1940

Dear Santa Clause,

I have been a very good big
girl this year. I haven't hit my 2
brothers over 1,350 times.

Santa Clause I want a 1961
Cadillac and mother said I
could have the Lone Ranger's
horse "Silver" and Tonto if
possible.

We won't have a fire in the
fireplace because I'm afraid you
might get burnt coming down it.

Mother said she would leave
you some beer an a jar of Rattle-
snakes for your deer.

With hopes,
Sue

P.S. Hope you make it, not really you but
the Cadillac and especially "Tonto"
"I just thought I would get my order in early"

Nov. 21, 1969

4:30 - A.M.   Lock Box 28
            One.   Pendleton, Ind.
                                    46064

Dearest Santa Clause.

        I'am in the
State Reformatory in Pendleton,
Indiana. I'am going to appeal my
court case to the Supreme Court of
Indiana. I' belive in Christ, god,
and Cristmas, Santa - would you
get me a lawyer, and the money
it will take to get out on a appeal
bond for Christmas.

        I'do so thank you very much.

December 24, 1969

Mr. Santa Claus
North Pole

Dear Sir:

With regard to my coming Christmas present, it is respectfully requested that
for my efforts in 1969 I receive $2,000,000 cold cash.

                            Regards,

                            Paul S.

PS:bt

Portgordon
Banffshire
Scotland.
13. 10. 67.

Dear Santa Claus,
          How nice it must be
never to grow older, I am 1 year
older since You wrote from Indiana
last X mas. You remain the same,
I have 18 grandchildren and
would you please write to
one or two, who still believe
in You.

          Miss Alison

          Peas Newton
          Chester
          England.

Dear Santa Clause

    I am in the first
grade, but can't write very
good. Mommy is writing
to you for me. All I
want for Christmas is a
guitar & a walkie talkie.
The guitar you gave me last
yr. is broken. My little
brother Bobby broke mine
when he jumped on it. If
you can bring them to me I
won't ask for nothing else.
    Thank you Santa Claus.

                Terry Joe
                Ireland, Ind.

Last May I was seven so I
am getting Lots older.
Have a good trip and I say
hi to Rhodolph since I won't be
able to see him Christmas Eve.
Yours Truely
Ben & Tom

Mr. & Mrs. Santa Claus.
Santa land Rd. 222 nd
Candycane, North Pole

Dec. 14th, 1968

Dear Santa Claus :-

Hello to you. I hope
you will not get the
Honk-Konk Flee. I try
to be good most the time.

Please do you have time to answer
me? Please remember my
family- specially - my sister, deanne
and me too. Love to you.
MERRY CHRISTMAS Betty

SCPL-6

Dear Santy,

My name is Kim and I am 3 yrs old. I have a little baby sister and her name is Sissy. We have tried to be good girls but sometimes Mommy says were a little bad.

Please bring me a Barbie doll and some doll clothes and any other toys you might have. Please bring Sissy a baby doll and some nice baby toys.

We will leave you some Kool-aide and cookies by the tree.

I love you Santa Claus
Kim

Dec 11, 1966

Dear Santa Clause,

I am not sure if I was a good girl this year. But if I get presents for Chrismas I promise to be a good girl next year. Here is what I want. I would like to have some clothes, and anything you would want me to have. And if you want you can give other children more toys then me. But there are so many more things I want but I can't have. Like beatles records, doll, roller skakes and a record player. But you don't have to give me all these things.

Love Always
Jofrances

40 kisses   XXXXXXXXXX
                    XXXXXXXXXX
                    XXXXXXXXXXx
                    XXXXXXXXXX

6. I will love you even when I'll be 40 years old, and its not only because I want presents Its because I Love you

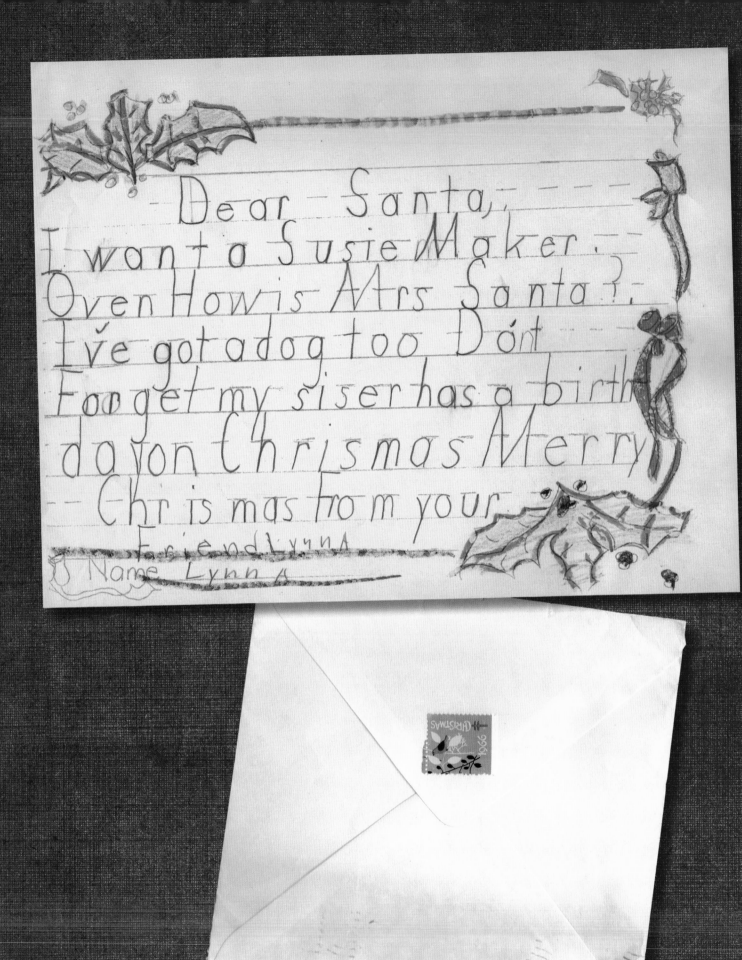

Dear Santa,
I want a Susie Maker.
Oven How is Mrs Santa?.
I've got a dog too Dónt
Forget my siser has a birth
day on Chrismas Merry
Chrismas from your
Friend Lynn A
Name Lynn A

Dear Santa,
    I Like candy Canes.
They are hot on your
tung. If you likeke
them alot they get
sharp if you poke
someone it will hert
and they will say Oche.
It would be nice if I found
a big candy cane In my
stocking. y

     Your candy cane lover,
Kevin

Tomah Wis.
Dec. 11, 1974

pal Fair Inc.

Dear Sir

My name is Kevin and I live at Warnke Road Michingan City Indiana

I am 11 years old and I was born on Christmas Day December 25, 1962

I would like very much to become an honorary mayor, fire chei for or a police cheif because it would be a great honor to me and it would be a great thrill to me to be one of them and it would be fun. So i wish i get to be one of them.

Sincerely
Kevin

Jeffery wants Tiger Cat for Xmas. Please bring it or Jeff will be so mad he wont give you any cookies or milk.

Thank you

Santa Claus
North Pole
Santa Claus, Ind.

P.S. see you at Xmas.

Dear Santa,
    I have made out a Christmas list,
but I can't find a doll I like. I would
rather have a baby sister, but I know
no matter how hard I wish I will never
get one (ever). So if you will look in your
workshop and stores and see if you can find
a doll you think I'd like I'd be happy. I
would like to have a 1 or 2 year old floppy doll
that looks just like a baby, kind of tall about
<u>24 or 25</u> in. (heavy if you can find one) I want to thank
you for all my gifts last year. I hope you
won't stop bringing my family and me presents
just because I'm in the 7th grade. Last year
when I wrote you the letter in my stocking
about the baby sister and you said "You
never can tell" it pepped me up for about
6 months. Then I began to think that I never
would get one because when I mention it
to my mother, she gets mad! If you write
me a letter this year will you put in it
if I will get a baby sister or not please?

    P. S. I love you. (I want you to come this
year even if you think I'm too old.)

XXXXXXX-000000   Love,
    XXX   000   Gail

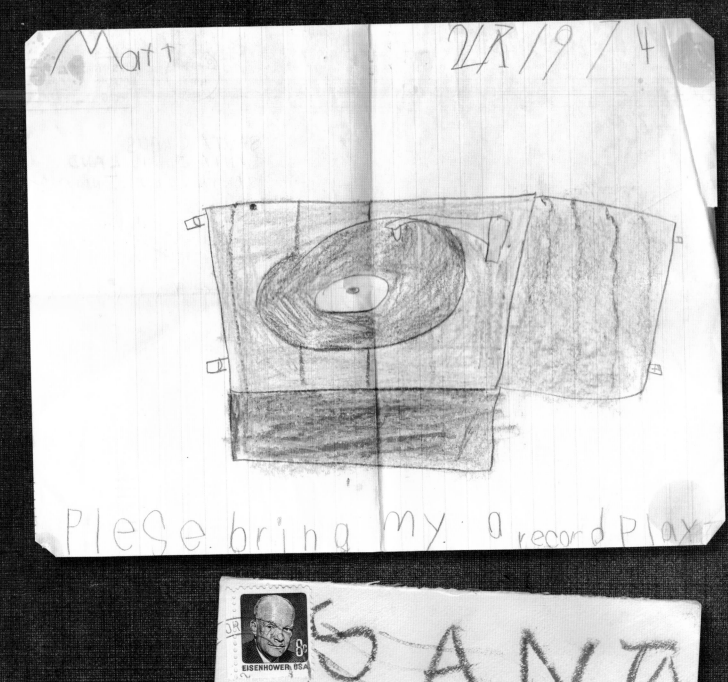

Matt   2/R/19/7/4

Plese bring my a record Play

SANTA CLAUS,
INDIANA, 47579

Dear Santa Clause

This is what I want fore
Christmas. I want a sleeping
bag, a pink nightgown, monoply,
bracelet, neckles, sled, a new
bed, That's what I want
for Christmas

Love
Debbie

P. S.
Why do you come
boun the chimney?

Answer

MEMORANDUM

TO: SANTA CLAUS
FROM: JIM
DATE: OCTOBER 30, 1973 AD
RE: ANNUAL GRATUITIES

Dear Nick: It came to my attention last year that I was in a low-
priority rating on your list. This I find to be understandable, as
there are many people who must be accomodated. Nonetheless, I feel
that such action should be terminated immediately if not sooner.
If your activities do not change during this year's worldly romp, and
I do not receive top-priority rating, I shall be forced to take the
following drastic action: (1) Your Good Will vending license will be

Mr. Santa Claus   -2-   October 30, 1973

revoked (2) Your reindeer will be exchanged for anteaters, and (3) your
elves will be requested to turn in their union cards and return to the
rank of fairies. Please give serious consideration to this matter.

Season's Greetings.

Santa Claus
36 North Pole Lane
Walrus North Pole
000010

NOV 29

UNITED STATES WASHINGTON 5¢

Dear Santa Claus,
    I would like you
to bring me:
        duna buggy
        sock em rock em robots
        astro space center
        tinker toys
        batmobile
        hot wheels
        johnny lightning race-
        track
        gas station
        big wheels
        helicopter
        airplane
    *   lots of candy
        surprises
Santa I have been a
good boy so far and
I will try always to
mind my mommy and
daddy

            Your friend,
            Floydie

July 14-1975

Dear Santa;

I . am only 76 years old, but I still belive in Christmas; and of our Blessed Saviors birth. Thru all the past years we in our family have looked forward to the coming of the Yule tide season. I don't expect much of the material things that was once our anticipation; but however give me love, truth, honesty Charity and the wonderful gifts and fruits of the spirit. Wishing and praying good Will health and happiness for all mankind.

Your servant, - Wilber

DEC 14 '70

1st Floor

Chicago, Illinois 60623
December 14th. 1970

Santa Claus
Santa Claus, Indiana 47579
Dear St. Nick,

We would both appreciate it ever so very much or also would our 8 children if you would please know hind or to worthy toy and help them out and surprise them with some clothing (2nd hand) and all of us with some food or canned goods for the Christmas holiday season. I'm the only one is our household working at the same place for the past 15 years. We do not own a home of our own nor do we own a love or auto. All we ask for is this food and clothing just once a year. We do not get any help or aid from the city. I'm just trying to do the best I can from day to day. — The children which we have are 5 girls whose ages are as follows:- 9 - 8 - 5 - 3 + 5 months. I furnish have 3 boys whose ages are as follows 12 - 7 + 2 years old. If you cannot fill out the above mentioned request then perhaps even a Christmas Greeting Card or a personal letter from Santa Claus would make them all ever so very happy and joyous. My wife and I both wish the of you. Thank you very much and God Bless You.

Sincerely yours.
Mr. Thaddeus (Ted)

December 12, 1971

Dear Santa Claus,

My mother is writing this for me because I am only 5½ years old and can't write yet. I try to help mother and daddy and have been picking up my baby brother's toys today.

My grandpa has a dog named Ding who is very old and I try to help Ding and be extra nice to him. Also I try to be nice to grandma's cat named Petunia.

I will try to be a better boy so I get the things I want for Christmas. Also I will try to dress myself and help mommy.

Please bring me a Screaming Demon, an SSP car, a space dragster, a Spyder bike, a fat track, some Hot Birds, a play gun that makes noise, some new Hot Wheels cars, a cowboy hat and gun holster set, some cowboy boots, some Dingalings and a lampshade for my lamp. Also a rocket set and a sleeping bag would be nice.

If you want to give some of this to other children it will be okay.

Please don't forget my little brother, Eric, who is 2½ years old. Also my baby kitten, Pyewacket, would like a bed, a scratching post and some kitty toys.

I will try hard to be good and not fight.
Love,
Greg

Oct. 7, 1975

Dear Santa:

We are twin brothers and we are five years old. We just started school this year. We like it a lot but we don't always listen to our teacher, Mrs. Klomparens. When we are naughty we have to stay in during recess and lay on our mats.

Our Foster Mommy said that if we tried very hard to be good boys maybe you would bring us some of the toys we want.

Scott's List	Jimmy's List
a wrecker truck	a U haul truck
a fire truck	Putt - Putt train
a motor home camper	Sit n Spin
Pajamas, Robe & slippers	Pajamas, Robe & slippers
walkie-talkie	Some candy

We will leave cookies out for you Xmas Eve.

Thank you,

Love

Riley, Michigan
49423

Jim + Scott

Dear Santa
Claus
I head on the news
that you had an
operation and I'd
hope you feel
better soon.
Tammy's my best
friend she is nice
and we invited he over
and we played
she moved away
and I miss her
very much but
we see each other
every week omost
but we call each
other omost every
day. I sure do hope
you get well soon

Love,
Dannelle

XXXX OOOOO

1980s

Dear Santa,

What I want for Christmas is a lego ship that costs a $100.⁰⁰. The ship is big, I want a ship. And if you have time put it together, 'cause for me it's hard. I would put it together if I knew how but it is hard.

Santa I love you, Santa.

Thanks for ship. I hope you can give to me.

JUSTIN

```
DEAR SANTA,
ARE YOU LOOKING FOR AN ELF THIS YEAR?  IF YOU ARE, I'M
AVAILABLE FOR THE JOB.  YOUR COOKIES WILL BE UNDER MY PILLOW
THIS YEAR.  THEY MIGHT NOT BE TOO TASTY, BUT IF LEAVE THEM
IN THE KITCHEN, MY DAD WILL EAT THEM.  WELL I HOPE YOU HAVE
A NICE CHRISTMAS.
                            LOVE JESSE
                                 IN CASE YOU FORGOT, MY
ADDRESS IS                  THOMPSON, OH 44086, HOPE YOU
HAVE A GOOD TIME FINDING IT.  JUST LET RUDOLPH LEAD THE WAY.

JESSE'S CHRISTMAS LIST

BEST CATALOG

PG.420 #3   STANLEY THE ROBOT

PG.420 #12   REMOTE CONTROL CORVETTE

PG.421 #23   REMOTE CONTROL ROYAL CONDOR CORVETTE

PG.419 #18   HOTWHEELS RAILROAD FREIGHT YARD

PG.121 #18 MIAMI VICE SPORTS CAR - REMOTE CONTROL

            DAHLKEMPER'S BOOK

PG.410 #7 SUPERIOR ELECTRIC GUITAR WITH AMP

PG.415 #4 REMOTE CONTROL '57 CHEVY

              SEARS

PG.235 #7 MUSIC WAVE AM/FM STEREO

PG.294 #1 TRAIN SET
```

Nov 28, 1983

Hello Again Santa & helpers.

    Its been so many years, since perhaps 1960 that I have written letters to Santa, at Santa clause, Ind.

    This year 1983 is no difference. Thank You for your efforts to bring joy to many.

    This little man is now 5 yrs old. and depends on Santa to bring him his most wanted toys.

    Santa's response to him will be greatly appreciated.

    Please send to
          Danny

          RIVERSIDE, CA
          92509

Dear Santa

where are You?

First Grade   Vidalia
              Lower Elem.

Dear Santa

I want a tape player and a
Pala Ubdle tape and a OOpsy
Daisy she cros and falls and
crys. I have been good. I hope you
can get me them. P.S. I want a
infant set for my baby.

Love
Trisha Ann

Dear Santa Claus
My name is Mark.
I am in second grade
I like to play baseball
and football. And I am
sick now today it's 11-21-89
and I have a
brother and sister I like to
play with them. I
have been working hard
at home making my
bed evry day. and
making good grades
in school. And doing what
my mother tells me to
do. And hanging up the
clothes. Get my mother
a nice skirt and my
dad some new shirts and
my sister new black
shoes. And my brothe the
Lynx for Christmas.
and I want a remote
control car for Christ
Christmas. Your freind
Mark

Dear santa Claus
Santa can I come up in
the sky with you can I
have toy's a lot of toy's
can I go up in the sky
if I can whake me up at
the time you come I will
be redy I'll laey out
cooke's if you will let me
go up with you do you know
my name if you don't it is
Kimberly Jo

by santa claus

SANTACLAUS

NORTHPOLE

Christmas USA 1981
Botticelli: Art Institute of Chicago

Dear Santa,
   I would like a Stomper
road for my stompers. And a
good old, real skunk outside
in my back yard. A good old
horsey for me. Mommy told
you I was a good boy. I guess.
I keed a new swimmin' pool.
                    Love
                    Gabriel

Hope Ind. 47246
Dec. 8, 1988

Dear Santa, I want
    I have been a very very good
gril this year. I want a radio, t.V.,
Clve game, Indiana sweat shirt, watch,
pocket rocker, tractors. And a puppy
brease my brother and my family is
going to mame it Spud Machenzie, +
cats. I want your picer.
        Your friend,
        Annessa

go to Mrs. John
son's house to
get me a
cat. She has
lots of them
. Annessa

Dear Santa,
please give me these
Toys. 1. boy doll with hair
that I can comb cabbage
patch doll 2. Pee Wee's
Playhouse sockes in
small 3. Pee wee him self
4. Pee wee's Playhouse shirt Large 5.
Hot potato 6. Twiser 7. Hands down 8.
Early birds 9. silly dilly 10. girl talk 11.
Nintendo 12. Magnadoodle 13.
Lost 'n Found's dog 14. real dog 15. tape
tupe 17. watch 18. sun glasses 19.
Garfied book and Telephone and Garfied
war 20. Checkers, Love kirsten,
21. a picture of you

DEAr SantA
I would Like to have A
mermaiD and I would like to have
StrAWBerry DoLL and A big
StrAWeBerry bAby and A
BarBie doLL ohd A tractor
I BenD GooD I will Leave
some cookie

Love Jessica

I Love you SahhtA

Dear Santa claus
I Love you very much. I
whached a show about you
and thay sed thair was no
Santa claus. but I beliede
in you. If you are really
santa claus could you get me
a baby alive. The boys in
my class sed that thair was
no santa claus my mom sed
that thay will disappointed
when thay don't get any thing.
You are my best friend I've
got

Your friend
Sarah

Dear Santa
    I am three years old and my brother Dave and sister Andrea are 9 month old twins I love them very much and I just want to play with them.
    Our Christmas tree looks like a flying decorated bird, because I picked it out and decorated it
    Christmas is my favorite day of the year, because I love it. My favorite is opening presents. this year I would like a bunny tail so I can be a bunny for halloween, Rabbit wiskers and a carrot too. I would like some marshmellows, I would eat them all up.
    Dave would like a nice big halloween pumpkin and a big Nutcracker.
    Andrea would like a nice big dome. She puts it in her mouth but doesn't choke on it.
    Mommy would like a nice big comb. She would brush my hair.
    Dad would like a cup to drink out of.
    How are Mrs. Santa and Rudolf
    We do have a chimney but we don't have a fireplace, so you have to come in the door.

        Good bye Santa

          Alison

Dear Santa,

How are you doing up there, Santa, I want:
    A skateboard,
    a remote control car,
    a doll,
    and a typewriter

remote
controll

Skateboard

a doll

typewriter

P.S.
are you
really real?

Love,
Nicole Marie

Dear Santa,

I want a Baby Skates and a few plastic care bears if you can make them. I would really want a baby alive, a furry kitten that runs on a battery. Thats enough of a list, pick out a couple of these, please

I LOVE YOU

Elizabeth

P.S. Please come early to our house because we have to go to Gronma's house on Christmas Eve.

Dear Santa,

I'm not going to lie to you. Sometimes I've been a bad girl. I'm very sorry. My name is Kimberly Anne Browning. I'm in the fourth grade. All that I ~~will~~ want is a fashion jeans Ken doll.

Sincerely Yours:
Kim

P.S. Some people call me Kim and some call me Kimberley.

1990s

Aug. 3, 1996

Dear Santa,

All I won't for Christmas this year is a time machine, so I can go back in time and fix all the bad things that have happened to me.

You are the only one that can do it because you deal with time on Christmas.

So out of the goodness of your heart could you make me one time machine.

Thanks,

Austen

Clark, N.J. 07066
December 5, 1995

Dear Santa Claus,
        On Christmas Eve hurry up
with those houses, because some people
like to get up early. In your hurry
don't mix up the presents. Don't eat
such a big dinner before you leave,
because alot of people leave out
cookies and milk for you. Make sure
you have the "Good girl and boy list."
Make sure you have the "presents list"
also. Make sure you pick the best
reindeer for your sleigh to carry
you up in the air. Here's some more
advice for you, Santa, have a merry,
merry Christmas!

                Sincerely yours,

                Lauren

Dear Santa,
Hi, my name is Kevin. Is it 1 degree there? Around here, it is mostly hot. I am in third grade and I am in Mrs. Camera's class. How do you make more than 1,000,000,00,000,000 toys a year? How many brothers and elves do you have? I have one brother, but no elves.

Your friend,
Kevin

December. 9, 1993

Dec 02, 1994

Dear Santa

Do you remember me? All of my family is going away. I'm really concerned, I'm at the mercy of my owners.

The 3 youngest, Michele, Tracy and Eric have left. They use to include me in all of their letters to you at Christmas time. And I could be sure that you would deliver.

How I use to look so forward to them coming home and playing soccer with me. Or they'd throw a stick and I'd go fetch. (Humans are so easy to please)

But Santa, they left me with these 2 elderly people, Chuck and Linda. Don't get me wrong, they're great to me.

But hey, what I need for Xmas is at least a year supply of doggie treats. You know, the really good ones. you know how I like those raw-hide bones. (makes my mouth water, just to think about them.)

Don't be to hard on the young-uns. They've been good, just busy. Well, again I'm at your mercy and believe me I've been good.

Sable

P.S. Comet is my favorite reindeer

Dear Santa Claus

I know I already wrote you but I just want to tell you thank you for the letter don't forget I love you very much there is one thing that I forgot to put in my letter I want all the homeless people in the world to have lots of food and a warm place to sleep and stay and warm clothes to wear

love, Sonnie Sue

Nov 8-98

Chicago ILL 60628

Dean Santa Clause's
My Name is Alonzo   I am
6 yr's Old and is getting The Santa
Helper To Help me With my Letter
To you Santa I Love writing you
But not all the time Wanting My Father
Just Come out of Jail and was gon 9yr's
and it Hard for Him To get a Job So well
you Help me this year I need School
Clothe and Thing's To Help me get
Back on the Honer Roll again so please
Help me with Thing To Help in school
and Clothes & food iF you Can
8 pant Coat 10 $ 4 and Santa
Keep praying My Father get a Job
So He can Help me I Love and
you and your Helper And please
Keep us in your prayer To
                    Love Alonzo
                    Helper ho (6)
                    SonyA
                    Bless you.

Dear Santa,

Hi! How have you been? This is my Christmas list. I want
Nintendo. I hope it is fun to be riding over the moon.

Love,

Nicolas

Bike
Legos
Pizza Parlor
Mad Scientist
Movies
Garfield Phone
Saxaphone
TV
Microphone
Wallet
Pogo Ball
Musical Instruments
Hands Down
Berenstein Bears Books
Metal Detector
Nintendo Game, Ninja Turtles
Joke Books
Cap Gun
Camera
Work Tools
Hang Man
Crossfire
GI Joe
Micromachines
Sleigh Bell
Snack Shop

December 1, 1991

Dear Santa,

　　　How are you doing ? How is Mrs.Claus doing ? How is Rudolph ?
How are the elves doing ? For Christmas I would like a Sega
Genesis w/ Sonic the Hedgehog please, and the Sega Genesis game
Streets of Rage please. I have some problems at school. Almost
all of the kids in my class believe that you aren't real.They all
think that it is the parents who give them presents. It is true
that the parents give presents ,but the fact is that you are
real. I hope you think I have been good this year. I will make
sure this year that I will leave you hot chocolate when you get to
my house. I may even leave you a surprise. Have a merry Christmas
and a Happy New Year.

　　　　　　　　　　　　　　Your Friend Forever,

　　　　　　　　　　　　　　Ian

Terre Haute Indiana 47802

North Pole
December 25 Street
Adress: Dec.25, Santa's Palace
Send this to Santa only please
P.S. Get this letter there before Dec. 23

How are you? How is Mrs. Claus?
How are your Elves? I hope the
reindeers are ready for
the "big trip".
I have really tried to be a
good boy this year. My mom
and I had to move in with
Nana + Papaw to help us through
some rough times. We hope
everything will be better so one
day we can have our own house.
Mommy has never had one.
I will leave 9 carrots for
the reindeers and some of
your favorite goat cheese for
you.
Love
Michael D.

call me if too
your not
busy   Cherton VA 23316

Dear Santa,

My name is Joey and I am 4½ yrs old. I am a good boy to my new baby sister Sierra and I am not going to push Delainy and Mia down anymore. I am not going to close doors on them too. I am not going to hurt them or throw toys at them either. Please tell Kiya to stop throwing toys at me and to stop kissing me because she has stinky breath. She needs to brush her teeth. For Christmas I would like:

A little puppy - who stays small
A baby kitten

(over)

A baby porcupine
baby squirrel
baby turtle
baby rabbit
Volcano Blowout
Batman toys
Men in Black - CD
Jurrasic Park CD
Learning School Set
Grocery Store w/food
Grocery Cart
Grocery Apron
Bristle Blocks
Lego Table w/Legos
Giant Bat (Like 10 inches)
Rocking Horse
Superman Ornament

Thank You, Love Joey

Joey

Glendale, CA 91208

2nd grade

December 11, 1997

Dear Santa,
I what my dad to be smarter.

Love Robbie

Dear Santa Claus,
I would like a telephone that works because ours was turned off. I want Gem, and the Rockers and Makie for Christmas. I don't know what my brother and sister want. He is 10 and she is 8, please bring them something nice. If you can turn our telephone on, that will be the present for my Mom and Dad.
Love,
Sabre

Dear Santa,

I am Cassie, I know my room is messy and I will clean it up. I sometimes lie to my mom and dad. Sometimes I don't do so good in school. So if I get cole I will understand. If not I was a Mr. Potato head.

Name: Cassie

Address: _____

City: Trotwood   State: Ohio

Zip: 45427   Age: 11

Santa Claus is coming to town

Dayton Mall

December 2

Dear Santa,
You're a really nice man but can I ask you something? Why do you give people coal if they're bad? Why can't you give people bricks or something? Why do you always come through the chimney? Can't you come through the door? or You could come through a window instead.

Sincerely,
Lauren

Dec. 11, 1997

Dear Santa,

I have been trying to be a
responsible person. I hope I
would get what I always wanted,
the thing I want most is a dog,
dog, dog, I know I haven't been
taking care of my Giga dog but
It is not real and a dog would be.
Santa, I would even trade my one
and only Mom for a dog. I know
that a dog would be a big
responsibility but I have been
bugging my Dad since I was
three and I'm tired of it!

Love,

Megan ████████

December 5, 1996

Dear Santa,
	You	better watch out for dogs
that are not caged. You might get bitten.
It hurts when you get bitten. I've been
bitten before. Can you please bring me "Light
Three" for Christmas. Thank you. Merry
Christmas.

		Sincerely
	Cristina

Ronie
Shannon M.S. × Santa Clause
Northpole

I love you
and no offence
but you know christmas
is realy for Jesus 3 not you, Sant Clause
Merry Chrithmas

Royal Mail
Santa Claus 0345 950 950
Business Services
Santa Clause Indiana

Santa Clause Town

INDIANA

U.S.A

Dec. 2 1994

Dear Mr. Santa Clause,
What has been going on?
Well just to let you know, I do
don't have a chimney. So I'm going
to tell you where a secret passage-
passageway. Its through the key-
hole. I want you to show me
your ffortress or whatever you call
it. I have a cool trick to
show you.

Date
December 8, 1993

Dear Santa,
I like wat you sent me last year. but this
year I want a New Stocking, I wish I clod have a
cat but My dad won't let me, I want to see you, I
want a New friend, I want a doll, I want a Puppy but My dad
wont let me, I want Ashley to tell me tho thithe,
and Grandma to come back to earth. yours truly,
(Mindy) PuPR

Bunker Hill, IL 62014
Thank you!

I been good!

Dear Santa Claus

I belive in you.

Can you answer these questions?

Yes / No
___   ___

1. What is my name _____?

2. Does Santa sleep with his berd
out side or in side _____?

3. Is my house made out of
brick, wood or is it painted _____?

4. Who is in my family? pick
three. Bob Gloria Mike David or
Ryan? 1._____ 2._____ 3._____?

5. Do you know what I would
like for Cristmas?

6. Well if you want to know
look on the back of this page.

I would like a nice watch, a scooter and a nsery baby and my last thing is baseball cards and a book for the baseball cards.

Thank you

for reading my

letter !!!!!!!!!!!!!!!

from your

friend

Stacey

2

Dear Santa,
I would like a TV for chistmars but
if it is to much it is oK. How is Mrs.
clause a how is the reindeer.
This might be the best christmas ever.
Love
Amy

P.S. how are the polar bears
P.P.S. how are the puffins,
P.P.P.S. how do you have christmas

A Lucky
penny

COOKIES

Arcanum, Ohio 45304
December 16, 1997

Dear Santa Claus,

Did you live when the dinosaurs lived? I want a giga dog. I want a barbie house and a puppy.

Love,

Jessica

Dear Santa,
        Will I ever get a horse?
Will I ever get a farm?
Could I get a horse and a farm
  for Christmas?   Could I get 5

                                  horses?

                            Please!?

P.S. How is Rudolph doing

My Wish List

Dear Santa

I'm trying to be good. Can my Mom come home from the hospital.

Brandon

Dear Santa,
        I don't want anything for myself
for Christmas. Give gifts to people who
really need them.

                                    Love,
                                    Kensington

P.S. Maybe a VCR. And could you get rid
of the roaches? Thanks.

Dec. 2, 1994

Dear Santa,

        HOw many houses do you have to visit?
DO you get Christmas presentes yourself?
I'm not trying to be mean but can I have
a good present and i'll let you have some
of my Holloween candy? Or, if you dont
wont that you can have a cookey and your
reindeer can have some carpites or anything
they want even if they want somthing else
they can have it. I wish you can bring me
all the Power Ranger toys.

Dear Santa!

Before anything else I would

like to say 'Hello I am

Arlene G.   of

Margaretha Home for the Blind.

Do you remember on Christmas

and happy New year. I want

to have a gift a small radio

cassette. I'll be glad to

hear from you soon.

Love, Arlene G.
                    (she is 9 years old)

Philippines

Dear Santa

My name is Melody and
I'm writing this letter becaus
I lost my job last year
and my children I got anything
for chirtmas my wish is
to be the best chistmas
since I lost my job please
Santa just need coats and
winter clothes   Boy size 14 pants
                                    L coat
Girl Coat Med Ladies   L shirt
        Shoes 8
        pant 5
        shirt Med

                    Merry Chirstmes
                        Santa

December 6, 1996

Dear Santa,
       When Christmas comes and you are running
around like crazy you can follow my advice.
① Do your job and get out, you don't want to run of schedule.
② Watch out for dogs.
③ Watch The Santa Clause, 20 times. you don't
want to do what he did.
   I have a baby cousin named Lauren. Can you get
her a stuffed animal?
   I want a real Buzz Lightyear. My brother wants
one too.

                              From,
                              Chris

The Mouse InThe House
By Abby

here is the mouse. he is not a ordanriy mouse.

Dear Santa,
        May i have a pair of wid leg pant's, Bead Magic, Beanie
Babies, Books and some dress shoes please. Most of all a very
Happy Chirstmas.

              Your friend,
                 Abby
P.S.
                        Piqua, Ohio 45356
Have a Happy Chirstmas to all

Dec. 12, 2008

Dear Santa,

I would like these things:

1. World Peace
2. My whole family to be there
3. Sick people to heal
4. Snow
5. 1 million dollars
6. Yoshi

Your Friend,
Travis

[p.s or Luigi]

[p.ss HAPPY BIRTHDAY Jesus]

©Ellen Crimi-Trent

a cat but I want a cat and dog.

    Sincerely,

    Megan

      November 29, 2004

Dear Santa Claus, Indiana,

  Does Santa Claus live in Santa Claus, Indiana? Does your town celebrate Christmas every day? Ho in the world did you come you come up with the name Santa Claus, Indiana? and   My name is Megan, and I love horses. My town's name is Scarborough. For Christmas I want a horse. I have

Dec.3.200?

Dear Santa,
For Christmas I want
a music notebook to
right down song idieas, beats,
and other things. By the way
how old are you,how old is
Mrs. Clause? Do you go to
the bathroom at peoples
house? Do the elfs work
all year or not? Do you
have a kid? I also
want a picture of you
and your signature.

Love,
Devin C

Dear Santa's

Thank you so much for
keeping the magic of
Christmas alive.
I realize how much work
it takes to answer thousands
of letters.
I wish all of you a
Blessed Holiday Season.

In Christ's Name,

Ayu

Landon   — 7yrs

Evansville, In 47715

Larson   — 5yrs

Evansville, In 47715

Dear Santa,

My boyfriend is going to Iraq. I would like it if you could take him some presents for me, I'm sure he'll tell you what he wants. Tell Prancer, dasher, donner and blixen thann for making it possible for you deliver gifts. he leaves april 1st so it will be christmas of 2009!

WRITE A LETTER TO SANTA

to
Santa Claus
North Pole

From Taylor

Dear, Santa

I My freind has an elf
and I dont have any freinds
to play with so I was wondering
if maybe every holiday
can I of youre elf's come
to visit please because I never
get to go to my freinds house
so I thought I could have
one of youre elf's and I
will write you every 3
days of how they are doing
And I was thinking maybe
for 2 days you could write
back to me and also
I was thinking one of youre
elf's could visit me on my
birthday. My birthday is on
october 13, and I was
thinking can one of the elf's
come every Christmas? please
Answer

Reed ky. 42451 from Taylor

12-5-01

Dear Santa
how are you I Live at
maine. what
I would like for christmas
is a Bike. Legos. and a
snow board. and a surprise

Love Jacob   I am
8 years old.

XO XO XO XO XO XO XO XO XO XO XO XO
XO XO XO XO XO XO XO XO XO XO XO XO XO
XO XO XO XO XO XO XO XO XO XO XO XO XO
XO XO XO XO XO XO XO XO XO XO XO XO XO
XO XO XO XO XO XO XO XO XO XO XO XO XO
XO XO XO XO XO XO XO XO XO XO XO XO XO
XO XO XO XO XO XO XO XO XO XO XO XO XO
XO XO XO XO XO XO XO XO XO XO XO XO XO
XO XO XO XO XO XO XO XO XO XO XO XO XO
XO XO XO XO XO XO XO XO XO XO XO XO XO
XO XO XO XO XO XO XO XO XO XO XO XO XO

Jacob

Augusta, Me. 04330

Dear Santa,

love,
Logan

My Letter to Santa!

12-6-04
<u>date</u>

Dear Santa,

How are you doing? This is some things I want this year. A Laptop, Hot-wheels, X-box, DVD, PS2 games, and Basketball/Baseball cards. Oh ya I want a Bichon Frise to keep my dog Casper company when we are at school. I will name him after you Kringle. I will leave Cookies and carrots on the bar. 10 carrots and one is for you, to cut down on the Calories.

P.S. Christmas wouldn't be the same without you.

Love,
Signed Elijah
Age 9

Dear,
 Santa claus.
I want a plasma flat scream
Tv. I have been nice all year
I just want to spend time
with my family. And I rember
your lack toase and tolrit so
I got you Soy mik and choclate
chip cookies. I will always
believe in you I put my
name neat.

            your
              friend,
                nora
                  2007

Nora

KATY, TX 77449

SANTA

MY NAME IS Robbie
AND THIS YEAR I CANT BE WITH MY
DAUGHTER RAVEN. SHE IS A VERY GOOD
GIRL AND WOULD LIKE NOTHING BETTER
THAN TO GET A LETTER FROM SANTA.
SHE IS 5 YEARS OLD AND VERY SMART
& PRETTY. I KNOW SHE WOULD GIVE
UP ALL ANY PRESENTS JUST TO HAVE
HER DADDY HOME FOR CHRISTMAS. IVE
                                    HOPEING
ENCLOSED A STAMP AND WAS ~~HOPING~~
THAT YOU COULD WRITE TO HER AND
LET HER KNOW THAT DADDY LOVES HER
AND WILL BE HOME SOON!
                            OVER

I KNOW SHE WOULD LOVE
THAT, AND MY GIRLFRIEND WILL GET
A SMILE OUT OF IT TOO!.
    WRITE TO
        ↓
RAVEN

EVANSVILLE, IN

    THANK YOU!!

        Robbie

Robbie
Indiana Department Of Correction
Branchville Correctional Facility
P.O. Box 500
Tell City, IN 47586

This stamp identifies this correspondence as having
been mailed by an offender incarcerated at the above
correctional institution. WARNING not responsible
for contents. Any enclosed money orders should be
referred to your local postmaster before cashing.

SANTA CLAUS
P.O. BOX 799
SANTA CLAUS, IND
            47579

State Form 49295 (2-99)
TELL CITY
DEC 6 01
IND.

4757340733 03

Danielle

Clinton Twp, MI 48035

Santa Claus
   Kringle Place
Santa Claus, IN 47579

Dear,
   Santa,
   I was wondering if I'm getting a red or orange ipod this year. I think I've been good this year. I have pushed my little sister Hailee a little bit, but I only did it because she leaves all her dirty clothes on my side. A lot of people in my class say that you are not real, but my best friend Emme and I belive in you. I hope you have a merry Christmas.

       sincerly,
       Danielle

The Big Red Guy
Jingle Bells Lane
Santa Claus IN 47579

47579/9999

Dear Santa,
   Hi, this Is Tyler, remember, the one
you gave the bell to? Well thanks. Sorry
I broke my sisters phone, it's just
that she left me to do all the work!
And, sorry I kicked her to, she makes
me so mad!!! Well I geass I'm just
going to have to dill with it. Well
what about you? Hows your christmas
going? Are you getting any new
raindeer? How tall are the elvis? Now
would it be all right if I ask
for some things. I'd like mom, and
dad to get the things they want. I
can't think of any thing right now,
but I bet youd know. And Santa, could
you right back?

           Sincerely,
           Tyler

P.S. Thanks to   reading my
letter.

Dear Santa Clos

I hope you were wornd abote globle worning. I hope you are fiting agenst it. At diner 5-19-05 I asked my mom what was that big chuck of ice. She said it was a glasher.Then she said that they were melting back there in the Nouth pole. I hope that most of the animals do not die.

Dear Santa
my name is Kayla.
I'm 9 years old,
my granny took me and
my twin sister in,
I know she's struggling
because she don't get no
help for us. I wish I can
get toys, shoes for christmas.

Santa please
make my
wish come
true.

Happy Holidays

Dear Santa,

This is my first Christmas so I won't ask for much. Although I'll only be 7 weeks old on Christmas, I'm still looking forward to you visiting me and bringing me presents. Please bring me some toys and a couple of books for mom and dad to read to me. I will leave you some cookies and milk in case you are hungry.

Love,
Kaitlyn

Dec 1, 2004

Dear Santa,

I love you.   I have been very good this year.   I can't wait
until Christmas!!!   I will have some cookies and milk for
you.   Here is my Christmas List:

Robert

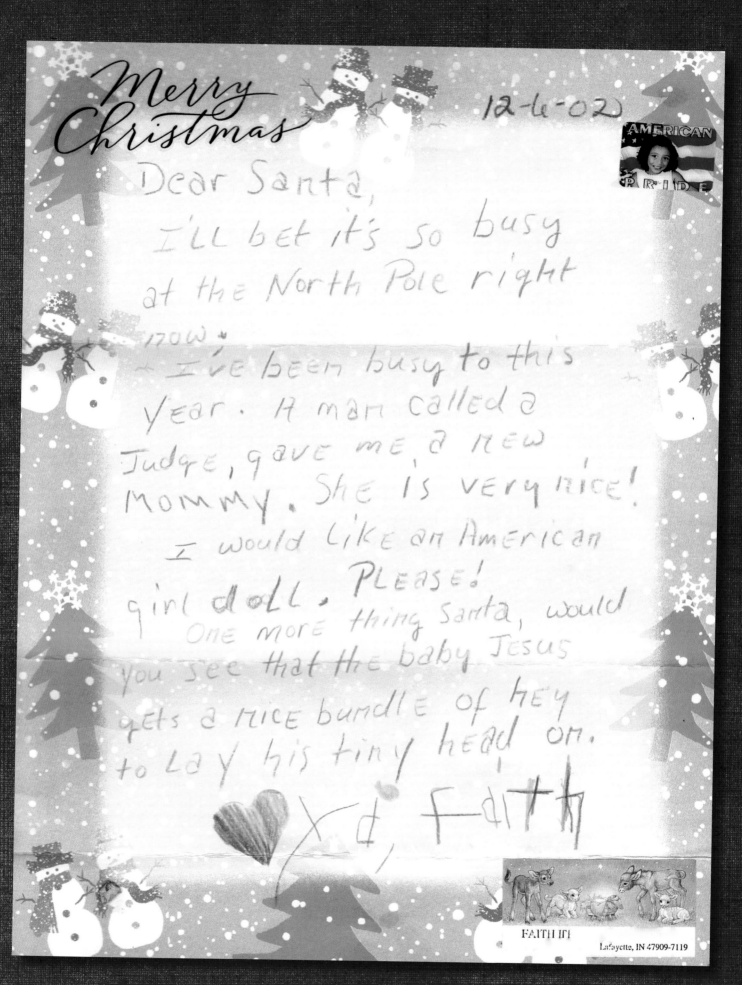

Merry Christmas

12-4-02

Dear Santa,

I'll bet it's so busy at the North Pole right now.

I've been busy to this year. A man called a Judge, gave me a new Mommy. She is very nice!

I would like an American girl doll. PLEASE!

One more thing Santa, would you see that the baby Jesus gets a nice bundle of hey to lay his tiny head on.

XO, Faith

FAITH IT!

Lafayette, IN 47909-7119

Dec. 1, 2005

Date

DEAR SANTA,

This year I have been good. You should come because I haven't hit my sister with my fourweeler. I would like a t.v. because I'm always bored in my room.
I would like a Nerf gun because my cousin is getting one from my family. Is Rudolph real? How do your reindeer fly.

Love,
Townsend

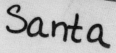
Santa

Our stockings hang upon a wall.

We have no fireplace at all!

You see the problem is quite clear.

Santa, how will you get in here?

We heard a legend. Is it true?

Of magic only you can do.

We'll leave out this little key,

And mark it "Santa" so you can see.

Your magic makes the key fit right,

So you can get inside that night.

Thank you Santa, here's our key.

The milk and cookies are on me!

Love

Jonah
Nate
Calvin
Duc
Ryan

Ella
Johnathon
Sophie
Nia
Adalise

Please put your name and address here

Branson

Valley Park MO
63088

Dear Santa,

I heard that you have gone on a diet of cookies. I will make you a ~~deal~~ deal I will give you 10 cookies for 10 presents. I want video games and a laptop. If you can't get that I want Legos.

Your Friend
Branson

P.S. I enjoyed the visit to Santa Claus Indiania.

December 6, 2001

Dear Santa,

I am writing this letter to tell you what I want for Christmas. My first and biggest wish is for the war to end. Next I wish the homeless people can find shelter. Then I would like for my brouther to be nice for wons. I want it to be the best Christmas ever. I am thankful for Christmas.

Sincerely, Megan

Dear Santa,   11-30-04
Is it true that you can't thow things?
Is the noth poll real? Are etls real?.
Are rain deers real? Have I been good. Is it
true that you can fly?

                    Your true friend,
                    Isaiah xxxxxxx
                         Ooooooo

Dear, Santa
I am sorry to
interupt you but
I just wanted to
know if I could
have one just
one of your
magical bells
off of your
magical sliegh.

          Love,
          Tristen

The NOTOMETER

Santa Claus needs to know who has been naughty and who has been nice. The notometer is a survey designed to measure how naughty a girl or boy has been. Ask your partner these questions and then calculate their naughtiness.

	often	sometimes	rarely	never

(1) Did you call people names?

(2) Did you swear?

(3) Did you fight with your friends?

(4) Did you bug your brother or sister?

(5) Did you hurt anyone?

(6) Did you push people?

(7) Did you write on the walls or desks?

(8) Did you argue with your parents?

(9) Did you disobey your parents?

(10) Did you break your promises?

(11) Did you lie?

(12) Did you steal?

(13) Did you copy homework?

(14) Did you cheat on tests?

(15) Were you rude?

(16) Were you impatient?

(17) Were you greedy?

(18) Were you stingy?

(19) Did you break the law?

(20) Did you litter?

Your Partner's Naughtiness Score (Out of 60):

Often × 3 + Sometimes × 2 + Rarely × 1 = ___10%___

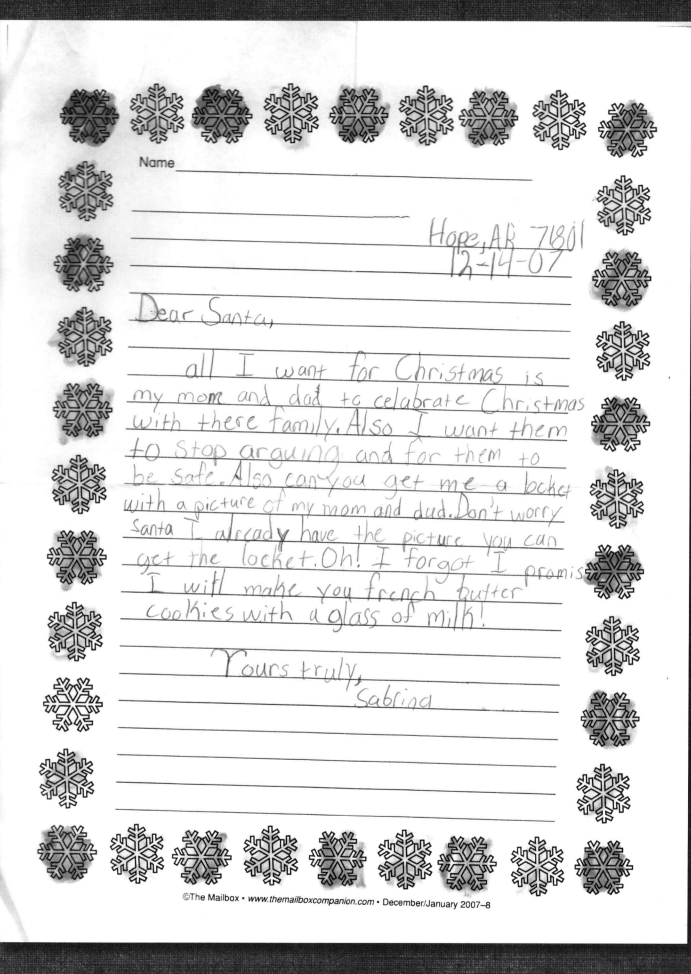

Name _____

_____

Hope, AR 71801
12-14-07

Dear Santa,

all I want for Christmas is my mom and dad to celabrate Christmas with there family. Also I want them to stop arguing and for them to be safe. Also can you get me a locket with a picture of my mom and dad. Don't worry Santa I already have the picture you can get the locket. Oh! I forgot I promise I will make you french butter cookies with a glass of milk!

Yours truly,
Sabrina

✱ List For Santa ✱

1. iPod nano (new) red name engraved
2. Barbie dream house
3. Holiday barbie
4. Car for barbie
5. Webkinz Seal
6. Webkinz Penguin
7. " " Turtle
8. " " Bunny
9. " " Lil'kinz Bunny
10. " " Husky
11. Deck the Halls DVD
12. HSM 2 DVD
13. The Game of Life Twists,
14. And Turns Game

American Girl →

15. Julie's Locker
16. Ivy's Accessories
17. Julie's pet bunny
18. Rural ballet outfit
19. Dance team spirit set

20. Julie's Day walking set
21. Julie's Room Accories
22. Julie's Sound Accessories
23. Julie's bed + bedding
24. Molly's Skating outfit
25. Samantha's lemonade set
26. Samantha's table + chairs
27. Samantha's party treats
28. Addy's lazy Susan table + chairs
29. 2 doll colonial carriage
30. American Girl horse
31. Elizabith's Riding outfit
32. Kaila's Dog, tatto gear
33. Niki Doll
34. Niki's Ranch Outfit
35. Niki's top + shorts
36. Niki's Straw hat
37. Niki's ~~summer~~ Ski wear
38. Niki's ski gear
39. Niki's Gala outfit
40. Let it snow pj's for girls

38. Sleeping bag set
39. Sleepover kit
40. Sleepover food + fun
41. Flip lounge chair for dolls
42. Velveteen coat set
43. Winter Weekend outfit
44. Licorice play outfit
45. Coconut & friend carrier
46. Bubble tub
47. Satin Floral pj set
48. Curlicue Daybed
49. Butterfly bedding
50. Spotlight stage
51. 2-in-1 ballerina set

56. Pretty Print outfit
57. Sweet Treats set
58. Sweet treats table
59. ~~Sweet Treats Bakery~~ sweet treats bakery case
60. Flower Garden Dress
61. Sweetheart skirt set
62. Evergreen Holiday set
63. Snowflake snowsuit set
64. 2-in-1 Green Apple set
65. Bows + Bunnies set
66. Ballerina-to-be-set
67. Bitty's Bouncer set
68. Cozy cardigan set
69. Baby's Stroller
70. Travel toy bar
71. 2 blonde girls twins

Elizabeth

Arkansas City K.S. 67005

Dear Santa:

Do be careful this month
and don't break your leg. I
wouldn't want you to miss your
trip Christmas Eve. I will leave
cookies and pop for you.
Don't forget a gift for Mrs. Claus.
I am ten years old and
have been good this year. I would
like the Millennium Princess Barbie,
Barbie airplane, Generation Girl
Books, games, Beanie Babies, Super
Nintendo games and any thing else
you think I could use.
I will like anything you
leave me, thanks.

Love,
Elizabeth

Dear Santa, Txt mssg speech bgins now.

Hope úve had a god year n ur toy fctry. Elves beingdi
Rndeer rdy 2 fly? Well, if you happen 2 noticed is letr np
escin, id rly appreciate a few thins 4 Christmas. Id like a LEG
O chess set, The Legend Of Zelda: The Phantom Hourglass game
for DS, Mario Party 8 for Wii, and Dragons ot Spring Dawn
ring book.

Sincerely,
Conor

Dear Santa. You Santa
dot have to
deliver anything
to me. I was
a bad boy i
Was trting to
be nice but
i coonet.

You Santa

roodof
the red nose
rain deer

Please accept this donation to help defray costs.

Thank you so much for continuing a great tradition!

When my daughter was a little girl (she is now 29), I helped her write a letter to Santa in Santa Claus, IN.

As I helped her daughter write a letter today, I couldn't help but remember the smile and excitement my daughter experienced when she recieved a letter from Santa Claus.

Many thanks to the employees & volunteers in Santa Claus, IN.

Since 1914 - Outstanding!

Patricia

"Nana"

11/26/07

Dear Mrs. Claus,
I love christmas and I want
to be pen pals with you and
Santa and the elfs please It's
going to be fun I can send
you guys stuff and you can send
me back somthing I want to
be friends with you guys and
I can tell you what I'm
like and you guys can tell me
what ~~I'm~~ your like. Do you
like shoping? Just wondering.
you

Santa   Jorell
               Marcia

               send me
elfs   back
       soon

Campbellsville'ky, 42718

11, 22, 08

Dear Santa
This year I would like a dell insporon 15
15.4 hi-def wide screen laptop. The price is
$479.00. I would also like an e-matic laptop
case. (It's only$15.00 so I can pay for it my self)
I also want a belkin f5d7010 wireless connect
card. , and is available at Wal-Mart stores it's
$29.96. , and I want a 2 year service plan for
$69.98. That's all I want for Christmas this year.
Oh and please email me

if the polar express
is coming this year.

Love
Tanner

p.s. if the things on my list are to pricy tell my
mom and dad to deduct the money from my
birthday and next years Christmas.

SANTA CLAUS STATION
BOX 9998
SANTA CLAUS INDIANA
47579 – 9998 USA

Dear Santa
thanks for the
Presnts But can I
have a Litle
snow? ♡ Amanda

Santa Claus
Post Office
Santa Claus
Indiana
47579   USA

Dear Kris Kringle,

If you would be so kind as to give all the Russian orphanages gifts. I would like you to do this because I used to be one of those kids and I knew how it felt to not have any presents. But most of all I want them to grow up like me with a family so can you give them cloths and outside cloths like pj's, coats and coveralls. I would rather you give them cloths and such than you give me presents and toys because thy are more important than me. So I ask you this all I ask you for now can you just give them goods and presents like pj's

coveralls

coats

toys

Sincerly,

a good kid danger

www.ActivityVillage.co.uk - Keeping Kids Busy

2010s   163

From: Anthony,

Pittsburgh PA 15224

Dear Santa,

I don't want much for Christmas
but my wife would appreciate some
lovely new lingerie ☺. She also
would love a puppy, nice and cute &
scruffy. I would love an 80" flat screen.
You're the greatest Santa!

Your Friend,

Anthony

P.S.
Help yourself to
the liquor in our
case... we have
homemade Kahlua!

Dear Santa Claus,

My name is Sharon Nicole
and Mommy says that I have
been so nice this year I
should be the Angel atop the
Christmas tree.
I helped Mommy without complaining
and did alot of shopping.
But I really want to ask how
everyone is doing like Mrs. Claus
and all your reindeer and elves.
If possible I would really like a
          Spider Necklace
          Night Gown
          Grape Soda
          DVDS

But what I really want is
something for Mommy this year.
She says that she does not have
a waist anymore so maybe she will
want that.
I really love what you got
me last year. I still use them.

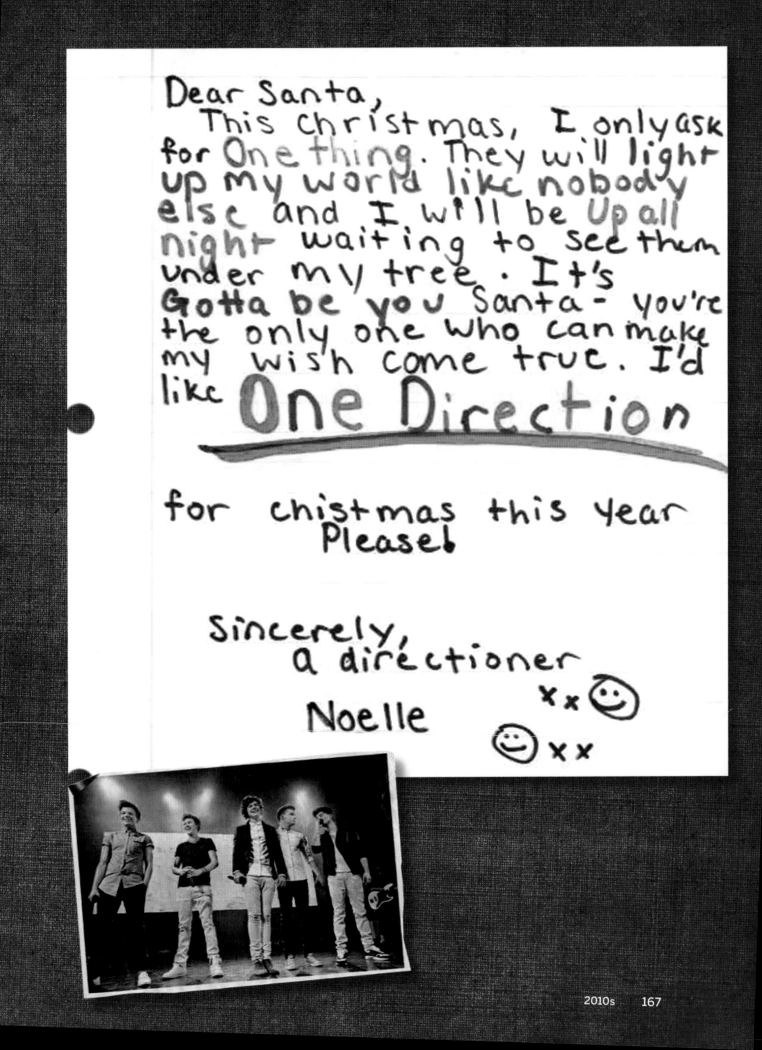

Dear Santa,
   This Christmas, I only ask for One thing. They will light up my world like nobody else and I will be Up all night waiting to see them under my tree. It's Gotta be you Santa - you're the only one who can make my wish come true. I'd like One Direction

for chistmas this year Please!

Sincerely,
   a directioner
   xx 😊
Noelle
   😊 xx

11/12/14

Dear Santa Claus,

Mi name is Yadiel ⸺ and
I am 4 years old. I'm from Dominican
Parents, but I borned in United States.
I wish you to give me something
for Chritsmas. My parents do not have
enough money for bay me something.
My dad is the only one that is working
and my mom is pregnant. My sister,
Yazlyn, will born is Chritsmas and I
will love if you send her something
too for Chritsmas. It will mean something
big to me if you send her something.
My sizes in clothes are the following:
Coats, t-shirts, swetters: 4t
Pants, pajamas, and interior clothes: 4t
Sneakers, boots and shoes: 11.5
I am a little friendfull (friendly)
and loving boy. I've been a
good boy this whole year. I got
good news for you, I can sleep
without doing pee in my bed since
June.   With Love,
                    Yadiel

Dear Santa

I am not eating
my boogers anymore
so now you can bring
me some toys please.
I wantie oat toy
that plays with you.

Thank you
your friend
Rayne.

Santa,
I've Been Good

Gramps

Dear Santa,

I have been a really good boy. Parts
of the year at least. I hope you forgive
me for egging and t.ping my neighbors house,
AND then there was that water bomb incident
at walmart, but it'd be better not to talk
about that... the point is I'd like a headset
with a mic as a back up. I promise I won't shank
anyone anymore.

Your Friend,

Alo k

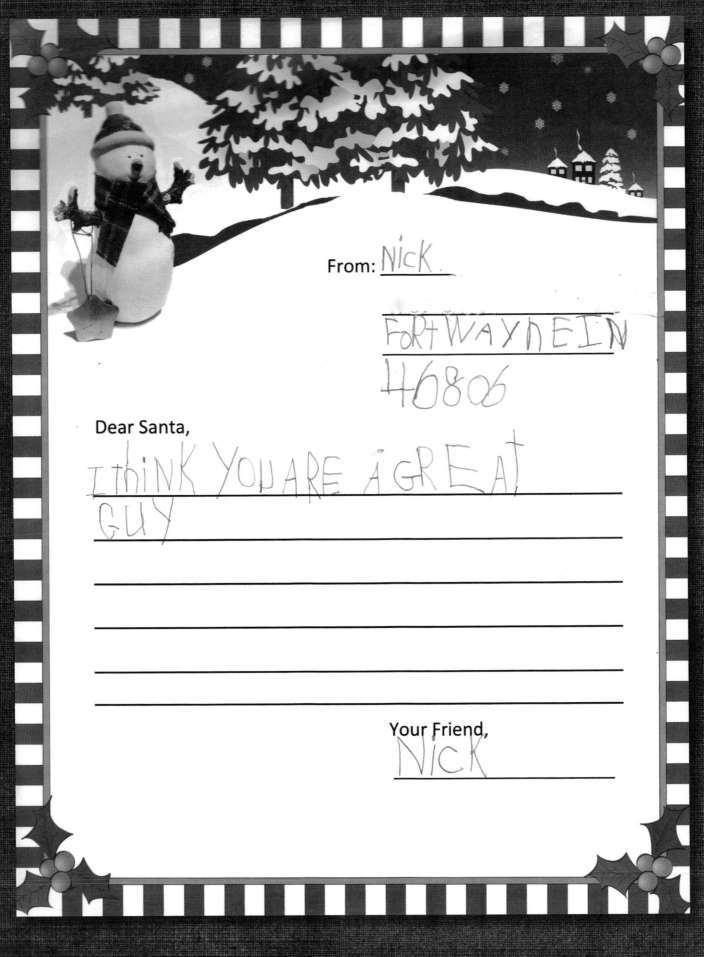

From: Nick

FoRtWAYnEIN
46806

Dear Santa,

I think YOU ARE A GREAT
GUY

Your Friend,
NICK

Melody

25620 Foucrerans

FRANCE

Cher Papa Noël

Je m'appelle Melody, j'ai 5 ans.
Cette année, j'ai beaucoup grandi
et je suis devenu plus sage.
Je me dispute moins avec mes
frères et soeurs et j'ai bien
travaillé à l'école. J'ai bien fait
quelques bêtises, mais tu connais
les enfants! J'attends Noël avec
impatience et cette année, je rêve
de trouver au pied du sapin :
Just dance 4 pour la Wii

Je te souhaite bon courage pour
tout le travail que tu vas avoir
pour Noël. Je t'embrasse très fort.

MELODY

Joyeux Noël

Dear Kris Kringle.
There is a lot I want this year, But this letter isn't about me. Its about my parents. They need a new car. They need it because theirs is breaking down. My dad gets a ride to work everyday, my mom can barely get to her doctors appointments. It is very hard on our family. Please. You are their only hope.

Sincerely,
Jakob

Dear Santa,
I want to thank you for giving me my
Grandpa back to me last christmas, he came home
Christmas eve, but sadly he died Jan. 1
But you gave me my speqil gift, my Grandpa
for christmas. Thank you. I live with
Grandma and we are OK.
ALL I wont is frozen shoe's and
a outfit. Thank you.

LOVE you,
Sara

I am 6years
now

Dear Santa,   Dec. 9
I was good. For christmas,
I want a real horse, water, a
Saddle, horse shoes, horse food, a real
Barn, a real hen, a real pig, a real cow
and to get my mom out of jail,
and 2 tikets to Pares.

from
Arianna

Craig
P.O. Box
Ironwood, MI
49938

Dear Santa and helpers,

   I have been very good this
year, I am axpecting a little sister
I don't want her, Mamy says her
will be fun. I heard girls stink.
I will trade you my sister when
she comes from the stork for a
elf, I want a race car and

a Garage set for christmas, There
will be sugar cookies and burritos
waiting for you, Thank you, Santa

                    Craig

Dear Santa,

It's that time of year.
  Here's letter number two.
Mommy's helping write it
  to send from me to you.

This is Alex
  and next year I'll be two!
I've made a lot of progress
  you'll be impressed what I can do.

I finally got those chompers,
  and I'm walking EVERYWHERE.
I think that I could use new shoes
  I have toys on toys to spare.

As much as I love to run & play
  and go out for a hike
I've seen the neighbor kids on theirs.
  I'd love to have a trike.

My Mammaw bought my winter coat.
  It's warm and black and red,
but if we get some Maryland snow
  I do not have a sled. :-

It's a good thing I'm a mover
  who likes to go, go, go.
Next year the Navy moves us.
  My daddy told me so.

But no matter where I live you know
  I'll always be your pal.
Will I leave out cookies & milk?
My friend, you know I shall!

Hugs & cookies,

Alex

Dear Santa Helper,

Thank you for what you do. Sitting down to write this letter & taking him to check the mail for the reply is my favorite new tradition. (I know it'll only get better.)
    Happy Holidays,
    Bambi

Crofton, MD 21114

© 2011 Fiddlestix Paperie™

Cara
PassChristian, MS 39571

GULFPORT MS
01 DEC 2012 PM 2 L

Christmas
Letter

BREAST CANCER
FUND THE FIGHT
FIND A CURE
USA   First-Class

Pssst!...
Look on
back

FRAGILE

Santa's Elves
P.O. Box 1
Santa Claus, IN
47579

GOD BLESS
YOU!

I'll remember
to obey my parents,
clean up, & pray

Dear Santa,

My name is Chase and I am 4 years old. This is my first Christmas without my daddy. He got sick and went to heaven in January. For Christmas I would like to tell him Merry Christmas. I have been a good boy this year. If it is ok, I would like a racecar with a pedal and steering wheel and a new book.

Have a safe trip. Love you,
Santa

Dear Santa,

How are you? How is Rudolph. I want a ventrilquist doll. I want it to talk to me by it self. Make it big. Make it a girl.

Love Lynnt.

Name Love Lynn T.

Dear Santa,
   Hello. I am 4 years old.
Thank you for getting me
a present. I love you.
I love you getting
presents to Maddie and
Cameron. I want to ride
on your reindeer, but
Mommy and Daddy can't...
they're too big. I want
to go on your reindeer
to Disney World.
I will leave you
chocolate chips, raspberry

May the season bring you the warmth
of friendship and love.

water, and a waffle.
Thank you coming
for me.

B E h

Dear Santa,

All I want for Christmas is
world peace, love and joy for
all mankind. If anyone can do
it, you can... or the Fonzo.

Your Friend,

Dan

Dear Santa,

All I want for Christmas is my two front teeth! I am 13 months old and still only have these two bottom ~~teeth~~ you see here. Can you help me, so I can Wish everyone a Merry Christmas?

Thank You!
♡ Julianna

IRMO, SC

Dear Santa, we moved & we don't have a chimney any more. Please come through the dryer vent. I'd like a toy snowman. Also a big fat dog to take care of my little dog and puppy. A PUPPY mom. I love my puppy.   Zhi, David

Plainfield IN
46168

Dear Santa,

My name is Julie and I am 5 years old. My Mommy says I have been a very good girl. For Christmas this year please bring me an orange doggie pillow pet, a Vtech Alphabet apple, and a swing for my room. Thank you very much.

Your friend,
Julie

Julie

✱ make my house messy.
get emma things too!
I will leave reindeer food out and
    cookies and milk.

12/25/12

Dear Santa Claus,
    I hope that you had a great summer. Since the
Hurricaine Sandy I am going to ask for much less
this year, so you can focus on the kids that
are less fortunate than me. My main thing I want
for Christmas is the PS vita with the "call of Duty
declassifyed bundle". I wanted some things
for the Xbox (If possible). It includes Assassins Creed 3,
WWE 13 and an extra controller (halo 4) speciallty.
I would love to get a Daniel Bryan red NO, NO,
NO t-shirt in my size (Youth large). If possible
can you add in Madden 13 for the PS vita (if
I get it (call of Duty declassifyed bundle, with
PS vita, and madden 13). For my stocking can
you add in NY Giants cards, accessories, etc.
Thank you for everthing and focus on all the
    other unfortunate Kids. Can you make the
Codys' Christmas Special because Mr. Cody
has been out of work for 5+ years so make
them have a Christmas miracle.

                        Thank you and please
P.S. I hope that you   write back.
are real & Believe ~   love Ryan

Dear Santa Claus,

Hello Santa Claus, My name is Sonic, I am a 16 years-old boy who come from Hong Kong. Hong Kong is a remote country that is locate in the southern part of China. I love playing computer games and programming in my leisure time. I want to know more about Christmas and hoping for your reply. This must be the greatest Christmas's gift in the world!!!! Instead of other experience or uncommon things be my Christmas's gift.

~~ Welcome to Hong Kong ~~

	sound
聖	sing
誕	daan
快	faai
樂	lok

"聖誕快樂" means " Merry Christmas!"

The boy who is writing a letter to you,
Sonic

Yan-Kiu So, Sonic

Ma Tin Pok
New Territories, Hong Kong

Dear , Santa

This year I have been a very good boy. I just wanted to ask how the reindeer and elve's doing? And, also, how do you get in my house? We dont have a real chimney and we keep our doors locked at night. Our fireplace runs on gas, and at first I thought it would make smoke and set off the smoke alarm, like my sister and her friend did when they lit to many scented candels... I will give you my Christmas list soon, and most of the things on my list are Minecraft stuff but i'm not sure if you know what "Minecraft" is but you probley will.

Sincerly,
Blake

Dear Santa, for Christmas this year I would like a 3DS with Mario Kart 7 for 3DS and Skylanders Giants for XBOX. If you think I wasn't good enough enough, I understand. OR, could I make it up to you by being good and polite to other people, (including Evan) from now to Christmass and then on? I'm very sorry.

check one

Yes   NO   Love,
                Max

Your the best, Santa!
   I love you!

From: Noah

Dear Santa,

I have everything I've ever wanted in one wonan

Your Friend,

Noah

Dear Santa Claus

My name is Rosetta and from Hong Kong. This is the first time for me to write a letter to you.

I am sorry that I cannot send a Christmas card for you as no one sells a Christmas card in HK. Maybe it is a little bit early to write a Christmas card. But, writing a Christmas letter to the Santa Claus, it is quite late I think. To show my apologies, I post a photo I took on the Victoria Harbor in Hong Kong at last Christmas Eve. I am not good at capturing beautiful scene. However, I still want to share my home to you. It is an extraordinary place.

For the Christmas gift part, I would like to ask for your reply. Santa Claus seems like a fairy tale to me. But in this year I will apply for the HK Auxiliary Police and this is my dream. I wish I could receive a Christmas card from you as a kindly encouragement at the Christmas!

Merry Christmas

Best wishes
Rosetta
24 Oct 2012

Let's have your happy time

with heart.

Victoria Harbor @ H.K.

24 Dec 2011

Dear Santa,

Thank you for all the great presents they are very helpful. I love them all. Take care of the raindeer. I can name all of them Dasher, dancer, pranser, vixsen, comet, cupid, Danner, Plintsen, and Rutph.

Love,
Chloe

P.S. I'm all wese in the Christmas spered.

Santa Claus (Pere Noël)
USA - Indiana 47579

USA

SANTAS ELVES
P.O. BOX 1
INDIANA 47579
U.S.A.

Julemærkefonden ønsker en glædelig jul, og takker for støtten til børn i Danmark.

Dear Santa,

My name is Briar. I am 4 years old. I have been a bad boy, but I am working on being a good boy. I kicked my teacher at school, but I promise I will be good at school. I am also mean to my big brother.

I will be good and nice. Will you please bring me a talking lightning McQueen, Dr. Playdoh set, legos, clothes, undies, and an ipad.

Hugs and kisses to you and Rudolph. I will leave you some brownies and milk.

Love -
Brian

fri, Dec, 17, 2010

Dear santa,
    I only want five things for Chistmas. Please make number one come true. it is most important it is for My DaD to come home. number two is for My mom to have the Best christmas ever. number three is so My Brother get a's in shcool. number four is so My sisterr have's the Best chistmas ever too. number five is for a new Book. christmas is giving, not getting.

(sorry I messed up on your hands) (and me)

December 1, 2014
12.1.2014

Santa. Maggie

Santa,

This year I have been... let's just say,... MEDIUM. I have been <u>nice</u> and <u>noughty</u>. *why*

<u>Here's some eksampels:</u>

<u>Noughty:</u>
- picking on andrew
- addatude
- playing tricks on andrew (again) :(

<u>Nice:</u>
- forgiving andrew for... EVERYTHING
- making breakfast in bed for mom/Alan
- not complaining while doing <u>DISHES</u>!! (Dad) :/
- Cleaning the <u>ENTIRE</u> house for mom.

So, as you can see I've been medium (behavior wise). So I don't want or need anything eksept maybe a...

APPLE GIFT CARD

That's about it

Sincerly,

(your favorite) :)

Авдеенко Варвара

220037   г. Минск
БЕЛАРУСЬ (BELARUS)

ПРИОРИТЕТНОЕ
PRIORITAIRE

SANTA   Claus
Indiana   47579
USA   (США)

47579✳9999

Olivia
age 4

Dear Santa,

Don't worry about me this year.
I already have what I want,
And she's standing right next to me.

Your Friend,

Taylor

Dear Santa,

I would like a reinbeer for christmis! a real reinBeer! and a sled pleas. p.s. mrs. clus I have not herd moch ad abote you but I'm sher you are very nice. I no that this is a little weerd but I love you santa your the best man in the whole world. and no it's not gust becose you give toys it's becose well, your a vary generus man that's why.

Love,
Jasmine

Hi reinDeer!

Hi Santa

me

Hi Santa!

P.S. pleas write

Dear Santa:

merry Christmas Santa.

Santa This year has been very
Tough on me alot of Thing's
happiend To me and my mom this
year. ~~and~~ were Trying our best
To mAke christmas a good one
for me and her it's Just me and my
mom her being sick and all make's
me really sad. That's why I
want To Try to mAke this Christmas
a good one for me and her so
can you please help me santa ⟶

all I want is a gift For us it can
be a small gift but at lest it would
be something better Then nothing
please santa help me mAke this Christmas
a good one for me and her Please.

merry
Christmas

Hana

Dear Santa =

Hello, Santa好 My name is Jean. I'm 12 yearsold. How about you? This is my first time to write a christmas card for you. I very like you. Hope you can visit Taiwan in the future. Merry Christmas.

MERRY

CHRISTMAS

Merry Christmas
Sincerely, Jean.
楊怡臻

Yi Chen Mu (Jean) Enterprise Co., Ltd.

Xinhua District, Tainan City 712

Taiwan (R.O.C.)

Santa's Elves

P.O. Box 1

Santa Claus, IN 47579

USA

James Martin stands in front of Martin's General Merchandising Store. Martin served as the town's fourteenth postmaster. His post office occupied space in the back of the store.

Photo courtesy Santa Claus Museum & Village.

Facing, below right: The giant Santa Claus Statue was built in 1935 and is twenty-two feet tall. The beautiful statue, dedicated to "the children of the world" stands at the Santa Claus Museum & Village.

Photo courtesy Santa Claus Museum & Village.

Postmaster Oscar Philipps served as the town's fifteenth postmaster. He helped expand the Santa letters program and continued the important town tradition.

Photo courtesy Santa Claus Museum & Village.

Afterword

DEDICATED
TO THE CHILDREN OF THE WORLD

"Dear Santa,"

is the way most letters begin. It is a phrase brimming with nostalgia, and for many of us, it conjures images of family, home, and maybe even a little magic. It whispers of the wonder that is Christmas, a feeling that resides in our childhood memories and that we carry with us into our adult lives like hidden sugar plums. Pleas, both plaintive and comical, all of them bearing the salutation "Dear Santa," are shipped from across the United States, emerging from small towns in the Midwest, wooded hamlets in the mountains, and crowded cities on both coasts. They arrive by air and sea, postmarked in storied European towns and on exotic islands in the Pacific. Children all over the world place their carefully constructed letters in the mail, confident that Santa Claus will heed their fervent Christmas wishes. But where do they go? What happens to all of those ardent letters? The answer, of course, is they go to Santa Claus . . . Indiana.

Make sure you put your full address on that envelope! Children mail a letter to Santa Claus.

Photo courtesy Spencer County Visitors Bureau.

A blizzard of mail passes through Santa Claus, Indiana, during the Christmas season. The Santa Claus Post Office, which normally serves a quiet town of 2,300 souls, processes over 400,000 pieces of mail in December alone. Thankfully, the whole town is devoted to helping Santa answer all that mail and to upholding a tradition that began over one hundred years ago.

The area was settled by German immigrants in the late 1800s, and the original town was known as Santa Fee. By the 1850s, it was large enough to apply for its own post office. However, the application was rejected; there was already a town with a similar name in the region. The United States Postal Department told Santa Fee, Indiana, to choose a new name.

What comes next is largely legend, passed down through the generations. The story goes that the townspeople were gathered together on a cold winter night, debating a new name for their town when a sudden gust of wind blew the doors open. The sound of jingle bells rang out, carried high and clear on that cold night air, and a child yelled, "It's Santa Claus!" And so it was. The application for a post office was resubmitted under the name of Santa Claus, Indiana. While the veracity of this Christmas tale may be uncertain, records show that the application was accepted, and Santa Claus, Indiana, established its first post office in 1856.

In 1914, James Martin was appointed the fourteenth Postmaster of Santa Claus, Indiana. It was around this time that the United States Postal Department instituted a courtesy custom of forwarding letters addressed to "Santa Claus" to the small, southern Indiana town bearing that name. Martin realized that Santa Claus (the jolly ol' elf) would need some help answering the letters that were pouring into town, so he took it upon himself to help Santa respond to the children who wrote letters. In 1930, Postmaster Martin and Santa Claus, Indiana, were featured in a *Ripley's Believe it or Not* cartoon panel. National media coverage followed, and the number of letters vastly increased.

Jim Yellig and his wife, Isabelle, began helping Martin in the early 1930s. Yellig, widely known as Santa Jim, served as Santa Claus for the region and Santa Claus Land. When the volume of mail became too much to handle, Yellig and Martin enlisted the assistance of the town, including groups such

Holly the Elf helps children write letters to Santa in the Original Santa Claus Post Office.

Photo courtesy Spencer County Visitors Bureau.

as the American Legion and the 40&8. Santa Jim ultimately served as the region's Santa Claus for over fifty years and personally answered hundreds of thousands of letters during his lifetime, scratching out responses when he was able to step away from his work at Santa Claus Land and from his appearances on radio programs and in parades. Hundreds of letters in the museum archives bear his distinctive notes, where he comments that a letter was "very needy" or simply a "funny one."

Subsequent postmasters in Santa Claus, Indiana, carried on the tradition that James Martin started, a responsibility that Jim Yellig considered his calling. Martin's successor, Postmaster Oscar Philipps, expanded the Santa Letters program and under his leadership, funding and volunteers increased. Philipps appeared on radio programs with an international audience, sending Christmas greetings from Indiana to listeners all over the world.

And so the tradition continued. By 1976, the post office in Santa Claus had moved several times into increasingly larger locations. Santa's helpers were busier than ever, and Postmaster Mary Ann (Schaaf) Long, with the help of Mabel Ryan, Jim Yellig, and Pat Koch, formalized the letter program under a non-profit called Santa's Elves, Inc. This organization merged with the Santa Claus Museum in 2006 and is today headquartered at the Santa Claus Museum & Village.

This story is unique, and the letters to Santa are a priceless resource of American history. They are a window into the past, capturing the hopes and

dreams of children and adults over the years, resting against a backdrop of national events that affected their daily lives. And while the specific requests have changed (kids rarely ask for a Shirley Temple doll or a Roy Rogers cowboy hat any more), the tradition of sitting down to pen a letter to Santa remains a constant. It is a garland string connecting each successive generation to the one before and serves as a touchstone for families and communities.

Santa's Elves recognize the importance of this time-honored tradition, a coming-of-age ritual in which countless children participate. Each December, the elves gather to help Santa answer all those letters. Some of the elves have been assisting for decades, while others are just beginning to help out. Serving as one of Santa's Elves has become an important tradition of its own with several generations of families joining in the holiday ritual. Local businesses, community groups, and individuals drop by during the day or in the evenings to answer letters, munch on sugar cookies, drink a little hot cocoa, and laugh and sigh at the crabbed missives stuffed in each envelope. Foreign exchange students from the local high school answer letters from abroad, responding in Spanish, Taiwanese, German, or French.

It is a festive operation; the elves often wear red- and green-striped hats and play Christmas carols. There is usually a fire crackling in the old stone fireplace, and Christmas lights twinkle on trees decked with homemade ornaments that were tucked away in letters sent to Santa Claus. The room is full of conversation and laughter. And if it sounds like a quintessential small-town holiday gathering . . . well, it is.

Each year the elves select their favorite letters and set them aside. Many of them elicit chuckles from the elves, especially those from naughty boys and girls who confess their misdeeds. It seems honesty is the best policy for these guilty children who come clean just before Santa takes to the skies. Other letters are sad, from children or adults in need of money or support or someone to love. Some letters are classic Christmas lists, containing ten, twenty, even thirty or forty Christmas wishes. And all of them touch the heart in one way or another. A selection of these letters is on display at the museum, though there are thousands more housed in the archives.

In this digital world, the elves remain busier than ever. They only accept letters through the mail—no email and electronic submissions for this group steeped in the tradition of pen and ink. Families can visit the Santa Claus Museum & Village, sit at antique school desks in the Original Santa Claus Post Office, and compose their letters to Santa. There is a mailbox on-site that goes straight to Santa Claus. **If a visit to Indiana isn't in the cards, letters can be mailed to PO Box 1; Santa Claus, Indiana, 47579.** They arrive through the mail all year long, picking up in volume after Thanksgiving, though the elves remind children over and over to get those letters in early. In 2014, Santa's Elves responded to over 15,000 letters at a cost of nearly $10,000 in postage.

My involvement with Santa's Elves started when my husband and I moved to Santa Claus, Indiana, in 2010. As a newcomer trying to learn the rhythm of life in a small town, I volunteered a day or two during the Christmas season my first few years here. But when I accepted the position of Director at the Santa Claus Museum & Village in 2012, I was unprepared both for the overwhelming amount of work involved in coordinating and answering all those letters and for the passionate commitment the elves hold in keeping the tradition alive.

I can now claim the pleasure of counting myself as one of Santa's Elves. It is hard not to be swept away by the craziness of the holiday season. Hanging decorations, wrapping gifts, and baking cookies are all time-honored traditions, yet the responsibilities and expense of preparing for Christmas can often make the jolliest elf say "bah, humbug." So it is a true delight to immerse oneself in a stack of letters to Santa Claus and read notes bursting with holiday enthusiasm. I've seen the joy in my own children's faces when they get Santa's reply—

Above: Head Elf Pat Koch responds to one of the thousands of letters mailed to Santa Claus, Indiana, every year.

Below: Joyce the Elf helps a child mail his letter to Santa Claus in the Original Santa Claus Post Office. This mailbox goes directly to Santa's Elves—no stamp or envelope necessary!

Photos courtesy Spencer County Visitors Bureau.

For those wishing to write a letter to Santa Claus, please address all mail to:

SANTA CLAUS
PO Box 1
Santa Claus, Indiana, 47579

Santa's Elves and the Santa Claus Museum & Village is a non-profit organization. The elves happily accept donations to offset the cost of postage each year. Donations may be sent to the address above.

For more information on Santa's Elves and the Santa Claus Museum & Village, please visit **santaclausmuseum.org**.

Thank you!

what an amazing gift to be able to bring that kind of happiness into the life of a child. It peels away the years and holiday cynicism, leaving behind a lingering reminder of my childhood's Christmas magic.

This book has been a hundred years in the making. The elves have always wanted to share this compelling collection, and when we were approached by Indiana University Press, we jumped at the opportunity.

We dug through dusty boxes of archives to showcase letters that haven't been seen in a generation. Several of the boxes were yellowed with age and contained letters that crumbled away at the corners when you touched them. It was a stroll through the past that meandered from the Dust Bowl in the 1930s to the war in Afghanistan in the 2000s. This book features letters to Santa Claus that the elves feel are the best of the best. Although it was difficult to narrow down the selection, we are confident that these letters will bring both smiles and tears.

The letters start arriving in January, and the elves always look forward to another busy season. Naughty or nice, get those Christmas wishes in the mail!

Emily Weisner Thompson

Pat Koch

is founder of the Santa Claus Museum & Village in Santa Claus, Indiana. Since 1943, she has worked tirelessly to make sure every child who writes to Santa Claus receives a response. Pat received her MA in Pastoral Ministry in 2002 at the age of 70.

Emily Weisner Thompson,

Executive Director of the Santa Claus Museum & Village, is a historian and author of *Images of America: Santa Claus*. She holds a BA in American Studies from the University of Notre Dame and an MA in History from American University.

EDITOR: *Mandy Hussey*

BOOK AND COVER DESIGNER: *Jennifer L. Witzke*

PROJECT MANAGER/EDITOR: *Michelle Sybert*

MARKETING AND SALES DIRECTOR: *Dave Hulsey*

EDITORIAL AND PRODUCTION DIRECTOR: *Bernadette Zoss*

PRODUCTION INTERN: *Katelyn Griner*

PRINTER: *Four Colour Imports*